THE DISPENSATION
OF BAHÁ'U'LLÁH

by
SHOGHI EFFENDI

A Supplement to
"Principles of Bahá'í Administration"

LONDON
BAHÁ'Í PUBLISHING TRUST

First edition 1947

Reprinted 1981

© *National Spiritual Assembly of the Bahá'ís*

of the United Kingdom 1947

ISBN 0 900125 46 2

P3

Printed by Page Bros (Norwich) Ltd.

BAHÁ'U'LLÁH

*To the beloved of God and the handmaids of the Merciful throughout
the West.*

Fellow-labourers in the Divine Vineyard :

On the 23rd of May of this auspicious year the Bahá'í world
will celebrate the 90th anniversary of the founding of the Faith of
Bahá'u'lláh. We, who at this hour find ourselves standing on the
threshold of the last decade of the first century of the Bahá'í era,
might well pause to reflect upon the mysterious dispensations of so
august, so momentous a Revelation. How vast, how entrancing
the panorama which the revolution of four score years and ten
unrolls before our eyes ! Its towering grandeur well-nigh over-
whelms us. To merely contemplate this unique spectacle, to
visualize, however dimly, the circumstances attending the birth
and gradual unfoldment of this supreme Theophany, to recall
even in their barest outline the woeful struggles that proclaimed
its rise and accelerated its march, will suffice to convince every
unbiased observer of those eternal truths that motivate its life
and which must continue to impel it forward until it achieves its
destined ascendency.

Dominating the entire range of this fascinating spectacle towers
the incomparable figure of Bahá'u'lláh, transcendental in His
majesty, serene, awe-inspiring, unapproachably glorious. Allied,
though subordinate in rank, and invested with the authority of
presiding with Him over the destinies of this supreme Dispensation, there shines upon this mental picture the youthful glory of
the Báb, infinite in His tenderness, irresistible in His charm,
unsurpassed in His heroism, matchless in the dramatic circumstances of His short yet eventful life. And finally there emerges,
though on a plane of its own and in a category entirely apart from
the one occupied by the twin Figures that preceded Him, the

5

vibrant, the magnetic personality of 'Abdu'l-Bahá, reflecting to a degree that no man, however exalted his station, can hope to rival, the glory and power with which They who are the Manifestations of God are alone endowed.

With 'Abdu'l-Bahá's ascension, and more particularly with the passing of His well-beloved and illustrious sister the Most Exalted Leaf — the last survivor of a glorious and heroic age — there draws to a close the first and most moving chapter of Bahá'í history, marking the conclusion of the Primitive, the Apostolic Age of the Faith of Bahá'u'lláh. It was 'Abdu'l-Bahá Who, through the provisions of His weighty Will and Testament, has forged the vital link which must for ever connect the age that has just expired with the one we now live in — the Transitional and Formative period of the Faith — a stage that must in the fullness of time reach its blossom and yield its fruit in the exploits and triumphs that are to herald the Golden Age of the Revelation of Bahá'u'lláh.

Dearly-beloved friends ! The onrushing forces so miraculously released through the agency of two independent and swiftly successive Manifestations are now under our very eyes and through the care of the chosen stewards of a far-flung Faith being gradually mustered and disciplined. They are slowly crystallizing into institutions that will come to be regarded as the hall-mark and glory of the age we are called upon to establish and by our deeds immortalize. For upon our present-day efforts, and above all upon the extent to which we strive to remodel our lives after the pattern of sublime heroism associated with those gone before us, must depend the efficacy of the instruments we now fashion — instruments that must erect the structure of that blissful Commonwealth which must signalize the Golden Age of our Faith.

It is not my purpose, as I look back upon these crowded years of heroic deeds, to attempt even a cursory review of the mighty events that have transpired since 1844 until the present day. Nor have I any intention to undertake an analysis of the forces that have precipitated them, or to evaluate their influence upon peoples and institutions in almost every continent of the globe. The authentic record of the lives of the first believers of the primitive period of our Faith, together with the assiduous research which competent Bahá'í historians will in the future undertake, will combine to transmit to posterity such masterly exposition of the history of that age as my own efforts can never hope to accomplish. My chief concern at this challenging period of Bahá'í history is rather to call the attention of those who are destined to be the champion-builders of the Administrative Order of Bahá'u'lláh to certain fundamental verities the elucidation of which must tremendously assist them in the effective prosecution of their mighty enterprise.

The international status which the Religion of God has thus far achieved, moreover, imperatively demands that its root principles be now definitely clarified. The unprecedented impetus which the illustrious deeds of the American believers have lent to the onward march of the Faith ; the intense interest which the first Mashriqu'l-Adhkár of the West is fast awakening among divers races and nations ; the rise and steady consolidation of Bahá'í institutions in no less than forty of the most advanced countries of the world ; the dissemination of Bahá'í literature in no fewer than twenty-five of the most widely-spoken languages ; the success that has recently attended the nation-wide efforts of the Persian believers in the preliminary steps they have taken for the establishment, in the outskirts of the capital-city of their native land, of the third Mashriqu'l-Adhkár of the Bahá'í world ; the measures that are being taken for the immediate formation of their first National Spiritual Assembly representing the interests of the overwhelming majority of Bahá'í adherents ; the projected erection of yet another pillar of the Universal House of Justice, the first of its kind, in the Southern Hemisphere ; the testimonies, both verbal and written, that a struggling Faith has obtained from Royalty, from governmental institutions, international tribunals, and ecclesiastical dignitaries ; the publicity it has received from the charges which unrelenting enemies, both new and old, have hurled against it ; the formal enfranchisement of a section of its followers from the fetters of Muslim orthodoxy in a country that may be regarded as the most enlightened among Islamic nations — these afford ample proof of the growing momentum with which the invincible community of the Most Great Name is marching forward to ultimate victory.

Dearly-beloved friends ! I feel it incumbent upon me, by virtue of the obligations and responsibilities which as Guardian of the Faith of Bahá'u'lláh I am called upon to discharge, to lay special stress, at a time when the light of publicity is being increasingly focussed upon us, upon certain truths which lie at the basis of our Faith and the integrity of which it is our first duty to safeguard. These verities, if valiantly upheld and properly assimilated, will, I am convinced, powerfully reinforce the vigour of our spiritual life and greatly assist in counteracting the machinations of an implacable and vigilant enemy.

To strive to obtain a more adequate understanding of the sig-nificance of Bahá'u'lláh's stupendous Revelation must, it is my unalterable conviction, remain the first obligation and the object of the constant endeavour of each one of its loyal adherents.   An exact and thorough comprehension of so vast a system, so sublime a revelation, so sacred a trust, is for obvious reasons beyond the reach and ken of our finite minds.   We can, however, and it is our bounden duty to seek to derive fresh inspiration and added sus-tenance as we labour for the propagation of His Faith through a clearer apprehension of the truths it enshrines and the principles on which it is based.

In a communication addressed to the American believers I have in the course of my explanation of the station of the Báb made a passing reference to the incomparable greatness of the Revelation of which He considered Himself to be the humble Precursor.   He Whom Bahá'u'lláh has acclaimed in the Kitáb-i-Íqán as that prom-ised Qá'im Who has manifested no less than twenty-five out of the twenty-seven letters which all the Prophets were destined to reveal — so great a Revealer has Himself testified to the pre-eminence of that superior Revelation that was soon to supersede His own.

" *The germ*," the Báb asserts in the Persian Bayán, " *that holds within itself the potentialities of the Revelation that is to come is endowed with a potency superior to the combined forces of all those who follow me.*" " *Of all the tributes*," He again affirms, " *I have paid to Him Who is to come after Me, the greatest is this, My written confession, that no words of Mine can adequately describe Him, nor can any reference to Him in My Book, the Bayán, do justice to His Cause.*" " *The Bayán*," He in that same Book categorically declares, " *and whosoever is therein revolve round the saying of ' Him Whom God shall make manifest,' even as the Alif* (the Gospel) *and whosoever was therein revolved round the saying of Muhammad the Apostle of God.*" " *A thousand perusals of the Bayán*," He further remarks, " *cannot equal the perusal of a single verse to be revealed by ' Him Whom God shall make manifest.'* . . . *To-day the Bayán is in the stage of seed ; at the beginning of the manifestation of ' Him Whom God shall make manifest ' its ultimate perfection will become apparent* . . . *The Bayán and such as are believers therein yearn more ardently after Him than the yearning of any lover after his beloved.* . . . *The Bayán deriveth all its glory from ' Him Whom God shall make manifest.' All blessing be upon him who believeth in Him and woe betide him that rejecteth His truth.*"

Addressing Siyyid Yahyáy-i-Dárábí, surnamed Vahíd, the most learned, the most eloquent and influential among His followers, the Báb utters this warning : " *By the righteousness of Him Whose power causeth the seed to germinate and Who breatheth the spirit of life into all things, were I to be assured that in the day of His manifestation thou wilt deny Him, I would unhesitatingly disown thee and repudiate thy faith.* . . . *If, on the other hand, I be told that a Christian, who beareth no allegiance to My Faith, will believe in Him, the same will I regard as the apple of Mine Eye.*"

In one of His prayers He thus communes with Bahá'u'lláh : " *Exalted art Thou, O my Lord the Omnipotent ! How puny and contemptible my word and all that pertaineth unto me appear unless they be related to Thy great glory. Grant that through the assistance of Thy grace whatsoever pertaineth unto me may be acceptable in Thy sight.*"

In the Qayyúm'l-Asmá'— the Báb's commentary on the Súrih of Joseph — characterized by the Author of the Íqán as " *the first, the greatest and mightiest* " of the books revealed by the Báb, we read the following references to Bahá'u'lláh : " *Out of utter nothingness, O great and omnipotent Master, Thou hast, through the celestial potency of Thy might, brought me forth and raised me up to proclaim this Revelation. I have made none other but Thee my trust ; I have clung to no will but Thy will . . . O Thou Remnant of God ! I have sacrificed myself wholly for Thee ; I have accepted curses for Thy sake, and have yearned for naught but martyrdom in the path of Thy love. Sufficient witness unto me is God, the Exalted, the Protector, the Ancient of Days.*" " *And when the appointed hour hath struck,*" He again addresses Bahá'u'lláh in that same commentary, " *do Thou, by the leave of God, the All-Wise, reveal from the heights of the Most Lofty and Mystic Mount a faint, an infinitesimal glimmer of Thy impenetrable Mystery, that they who have recognized the radiance of the Sinaic Splendour may faint away and die as they catch a lightning glimpse of the fierce and crimson Light that envelops Thy Revelation.*"

As a further testimony to the greatness of the Revelation identified with Bahá'u'lláh may be cited the following extracts from a Tablet addressed by 'Abdu'l-Bahá to an eminent Zoroastrian follower of the Faith : " *Thou hadst written that in the sacred books of the followers of Zoroaster it is written that in the latter days, in three separate Dispensations, the sun must needs be brought to a standstill. In the first Dispensation, it is predicted, the sun will remain motionless for ten days ; in the second for twice that time ; in the third for no less than one whole month. The interpretation of this prophecy is this : the first Dispensation to which it refers is the Muhammadan Dispensation during which the Sun of Truth stood still for ten days. Each day is reckoned as one century. The Muhammadan Dispensation must have, therefore, lasted no less than one thousand years, which is precisely the period that has elapsed from the setting of the Star of the Imamate to the advent of the Dispensation proclaimed by the Báb. The second Dispensation referred to in this prophecy is the one inaugurated by the Báb Himself, which began in the year 1260 A.H. and was brought to a close in the year 1280 A.H. As to the third Dispensation — the Revelation proclaimed by Bahá'u'lláh — inasmuch as the Sun of Truth when attaining that station shineth in the plenitude of its meridian splendour its duration hath been fixed for a period of one whole month, which is the maximum time taken by the sun to pass through a sign of the Zodiac. From this thou canst imagine the magnitude of the Bahá'í cycle — a cycle that must extend over a period of at least five hundred thousand years."*

From the text of this explicit and authoritative interpretation of so ancient a prophecy it is evident how necessary it is for every faithful follower of the Faith to accept the divine origin and uphold the independent status of the Muḥammadan Dispensation. The validity of the Imamate is, moreover, implicitly recognized in these same passages — that divinely-appointed institution of whose most distinguished member the Báb Himself was a lineal descendant, and which continued for a period of no less than two hundred and sixty years to be the chosen recipient of the guidance of the Almighty and the repository of one of the two most precious legacies of Islám.

This same prophecy, we must furthermore recognize, attests the independent character of the Bábí Dispensation and corroborates indirectly the truth that in accordance with the principle of progressive revelation every Manifestation of God must needs vouchsafe to the peoples of His day a measure of divine guidance ampler than any which a preceding and less receptive age could have received or appreciated. For this reason, and not for any superior merit which the Bahá'í Faith may be said to inherently possess, does this prophecy bear witness to the unrivalled power and glory with which the Dispensation of Bahá'u'lláh has been invested — a Dispensation the potentialities of which we are but beginning to perceive and the full range of which we can never determine.

The Faith of Bahá'u'lláh should indeed be regarded, if we wish to be faithful to the tremendous implications of its message, as the culmination of a cycle, the final stage in a series of successive, of preliminary and progressive revelations. These, beginning with Adam and ending with the Báb, have paved the way and anticipated with an ever-increasing emphasis the advent of that Day of Days in which He Who is the Promise of All Ages should be made manifest.

To this truth the utterances of Bahá'u'lláh abundantly testify. A mere reference to the claims which, in vehement language and with compelling power, He Himself has repeatedly advanced cannot but fully demonstrate the character of the Revelation of which He was the chosen bearer. To the words that have streamed from His pen — the fountainhead of so impetuous a Revelation — we should, therefore, direct our attention if we wish to obtain a clearer understanding of its importance and meaning. Whether in His assertion of the unprecedented claim He has advanced, or in His allusions to the mysterious forces He has released, whether in such passages as extol the glories of His long-awaited Day, or magnify the station which they who have recognized its hidden virtues will attain, Bahá'u'lláh and, to an almost equal extent, the Báb and 'Abdu'l-Bahá, have bequeathed to posterity mines of such inestimable wealth as none of us who belong to this generation can befittingly estimate. Such testimonies bearing on this theme are impregnated with such power and reveal such beauty as only those who are versed in the languages in which they were originally revealed can claim to have sufficiently appreciated. So numerous are these testimonies that a whole volume would be required to be written in order to compile the most outstanding among them. All I can venture to attempt at present is to share with you only such passages as I have been able to glean from His voluminous writings.

" *I testify before God*," proclaims Bahá'u'lláh, " *to the greatness, the inconceivable greatness of this Revelation. Again and again have We in most of Our Tablets borne witness to this truth, that mankind may be roused from its heedlessness.*" " *In this most mighty Revelation,*" He unequivocally announces, " *all the Dispensations of the past have attained their highest, their final consummation.*" " *That which hath been made manifest in this pre-eminent, this most exalted Revelation, stands unparalleled in the annals of the past, nor willl future ages witness its like."* " *He it is,*" referring to Himself He further proclaims, " *Who in the Old Testament hath been named Jehovah, Who in the Gospel hath been designated as the Spirit of Truth, and in the Qur'án acclaimed as the Great Announcement.*" " *But for Him no Divine Messenger would have been invested with the robe of prophethood, nor would any of the sacred scriptures have been revealed. To this bear witness all created things.*" " *The word which the one true God uttereth in this day, though that word be the most familiar and commonplace of terms, is invested with supreme, with unique distinction.*" " *The generality of mankind is still immature. Had it acquired sufficient capacity We would have bestowed upon it so great a measure of Our knowledge that all who dwell on earth and in heaven would have found themselves, by virtue of the grace streaming from Our Pen, completely independent of all knowledge save the knowledge of God, and would have been securely established upon the throne of abiding tranquillity.*" " *The Pen of Holiness, I solemnly affirm before God, hath writ upon My snow-white brow and in characters of effulgent glory these glowing, these musk-scented and holy words : ' Behold ye that dwell on earth, and ye denizens of heaven, bear witness, He in truth is your Well-Beloved. He it is Whose like the world of creation hath not seen, He Whose ravishing beauty hath delighted the eye of God, the Ordainer, the All-Powerful, the Incomparable ! ' "*

" *Followers of the Gospel,*" Bahá'u'lláh addressing the whole of Christendom exclaims, " *behold the gates of heaven are flung open. He that had ascended unto it is now come. Give ear to His voice calling aloud over land and sea, announcing to all mankind the advent of this Revelation — a Revelation through the agency of which the Tongue of Grandeur is now proclaiming : ' Lo, the sacred Pledge hath been fulfilled, for He, the Promised One, is come ! ' "* "*The voice of the Son of Man is calling aloud from the sacred vale: ' Here am I, here am I, O God my God ! ' . . . whilst from the Burning Bush breaketh forth the cry: 'Lo, the Desire of the world is made manifest in His transcendent glory ! ' The Father hath come. That which ye were promised in the Kingdom of God is fulfilled. This is the Word which the Son veiled when He said to those around Him that at that time they could not bear it . . . Verily the Spirit of Truth is come to guide you unto all truth . . . He is the One Who glorified the Son and exalted His Cause . . ."* " *The Comforter Whose advent all the scriptures have promised is now come that He may reveal unto you all knowledge and wisdom. Seek Him over the entire surface of the earth, haply ye may find Him.*"

" *Call out to Zion, O Carmel,*" writes Bahá'u'lláh, " *and announce the joyful tidings :* ' *He that was hidden from mortal eyes is come ! His all-conquering sovereignty is manifest ; His all-encompassing splendour is revealed . . . Hasten forth and circumambulate the City of God that hath descended from heaven — the celestial Kaaba round which have circled in adoration the favoured of God, the pure in heart and the company of the most exalted angels.*' " " *I am the One,*" He in another connection affirms, " *Whom the tongue of Isaiah hath extolled, the One with Whose name both the Torah and the Evangel were adorned.*" " *The glory of Sinai hath hastened to circle round the Day-spring of this Revelation, while from the heights of the Kingdom the voice of the Son of God is heard proclaiming :* ' *Bestir yourselves, ye proud ones of the earth, and hasten ye towards Him.*' *Carmel hath in this day hastened in longing adoration to attain His court, whilst from the heart of Zion there cometh the cry :* ' *The promise of all ages is now fulfilled. That which had been announced in the holy writ of God, the Beloved, the Most High, is made manifest.*' " " *Hijáz is astir by the breeze announcing the tidings of joyous reunion.* ' *Praise be to Thee,*' *We hear her exclaim,* ' *O my Lord, the Most High. I was dead through my separation from Thee ; the breeze laden with the fragrance of Thy presence hath brought me back to life. Happy is he that turneth unto Thee, and woe betide the erring.*' " " *By the one true God, Elijah hath hastened unto My court and hath circumambulated in the day-time and in the night-season My throne of glory.*" " *Solomon in all his majesty circles in adoration around Me in this day, uttering this most exalted word :* ' *I have turned my face towards Thy face, O Thou omnipotent Ruler of the world ! I am wholly detached from all things pertaining unto me, and yearn for that which Thou dost possess.*' " " *Had Muḥam-*

mad, the Apostle of God, attained this Day." Bahá'u'lláh writes in a Tablet revealed on the eve of His banishment to the penal colony of 'Akká, " *He would have exclaimed : ' I have truly recognised Thee, O Thou the Desire of the Divine Messengers ! ' Had Abraham attained it, He too, falling prostrate upon the ground, and in the utmost lowliness before the Lord thy God, would have cried : ' Mine heart is filled with peace, O Thou Lord of all that is in heaven and on earth ! I testify that Thou hast unveiled before mine eyes all ,he glory of Thy power and the full majesty of Thy law ! '* . . . *Had Moses Himself attained it, He, likewise, would have raised His voice saying : ' All praise be to Thee for having lifted upon me the light of Thy countenance and enrolled me among them that have been privileged to behold Thy face ! ' *" " *North and South both vibrate to the call announcing the advent of our Revelation. We can hear the voice of Mecca acclaiming : ' All praise be to Thee, O Lord my God, the All-Glorious, for having wafted over me the breath redolent with the fragrance of Thy presence ! ' Jerusalem, likewise, is calling aloud : ' Lauded and magnified art Thou, O Beloved of earth and heaven, for having turned the agony of my separation from Thee into the joy of a life-giving reunion ! ' *"

" *By the righteousness of God,*" Bahá'u'lláh wishing to reveal the full potency of His invincible power asserts, " *should a man, all alone, arise in the name of Bahá and put on the armour of His love, him will the Almighty cause to be victorious, though the forces of earth and heaven be arrayed against him.*" " *By God besides Whom is none other God ! Should any one arise for the triumph of our Cause, him will God render victorious though tens of thousands of enemies be leagued against him. And if his love for Me wax stronger, God will establish his ascendency over all the powers of earth and heaven. Thus have We breathed the spirit of power into all regions.*"

" *This is the King of Days,*" He thus extols the age that has witnessed the advent of His Revelation, " *the Day that hath seen the coming of the Best-beloved, Him Who through all eternity hath been acclaimed the Desire of the World.*" " *The world of being shineth in this Day with the resplendency of this Divine Revelation.*

All created things extol its saving grace and sing its praises. The universe is wrapt in an ecstasy of joy and gladness. The Scriptures of past Dispensations celebrate the great jubilee that must needs greet this most great Day of God. Well is it with him that hath lived to see this Day and hath recognized its station." " Were mankind to give heed in a befitting manner to no more than one word of such a praise it would be so filled with delight as to be overpowered and lost in wonder. Entranced, it would then shine forth resplendent above the horizon of true understanding."

" *Be fair, ye peoples of the world;*" He thus appeals to mankind, " *is it meet and seemly for you to question the authority of one Whose presence ' He Who conversed with God ' (Moses) hath longed to attain, the beauty of Whose countenance ' God's Well-beloved ' (Muḥammad) had yearned to behold, through the potency of Whose love the ' Spirit of God ' (Jesus) ascended to heaven, for Whose sake the ' Primal Point ' (the Báb) offered up His life ? " " Seize your chance,*" He admonishes His followers, " *inasmuch as a fleeting moment in this Day excelleth centuries of a bygone age . . . Neither sun nor moon hath witnessed a day such as this . . . It is evident that every age in which a Manifestation of God hath lived is divinely ordained and may, in a sense, be characterized as God's appointed Day. This Day, however, is unique and is to be distinguished from those that have preceded it. The designation ' Seal of the Prophets ' fully reveals and demonstrates its high station.*"

Expatiating on the forces latent in His Revelation Bahá'u'lláh reveals the following : " *Through the movement of Our Pen of glory We have, at the bidding of the omnipotent Ordainer, breathed a new life into every human frame and instilled into every word a fresh potency. All created things proclaim the evidences of this worldwide regeneration.*" " *This is,*" He adds, " *the most great, the most joyful tidings imparted by the pen of this wronged One to mankind.*" " *How great,*" He in another passage exclaims, " *is the Cause ! How staggering the weight of its message ! This is the Day of which it hath been said : ' O my son ! verily God will bring everything to light though it were but the weight of a grain of mustard seed, and hidden in a rock, or in the heavens or in the earth ; for God is* *subtile, informed of all.'" " By the righteousness of the one true God ! If one speck of a jewel be lost and buried beneath a mountain of stones, and lie hidden beyond the seven seas, the Hand of Omnipotence will assuredly reveal it in this day, pure and cleansed from dross."* " He that partaketh of the waters of My Revelation will taste all the incorruptible delights ordained by God from the beginning that hath no beginning to the end that hath no end." " Every single letter proceeding from Our mouth is endowed with such regenerative power as to enable it to bring into existence a new creation — a creation the magnitude of which is inscrutable to all save God. He verily hath knowledge of all things." " It is in Our power, should We wish it, to enable a speck of floating dust to generate, in less than the twinkling of an eye, suns of infinite, of unimaginable splendour, to cause a dewdrop to develop into vast and numberless oceans, to infuse into every letter such a force as to empower it to unfold all the knowledge of past and future ages." " We are possessed of such power which, if brought to light, will transmute the most deadly of poisons into a panacea of unfailing efficacy."*

Estimating the station of the true believer He remarks : " *By the sorrows which afflict the beauty of the All-Glorious ! Such is the station ordained for the true believer that if to an extent smaller than a needle's eye the glory of that station were to be unveiled to mankind, every beholder would be consumed away in his longing to attain it. For this reason it hath been decreed that in this earthly life the full measure of the glory of his own station should remain concealed from the eyes of such a believer."* " *If the veil be lifted,"* He similarly affirms, " *and the full glory of the station of those who have turned wholly towards God, and in their love for Him renounced the world, be made manifest, the entire creation would be dumbfounded."*

Stressing the superlative character of His Revelation as compared with the Dispensation preceding it, Bahá'u'lláh makes the following affirmation : " *If all the peoples of the world be invested with the powers and attributes destined for the Letters of the Living, the Báb's chosen disciples, whose station is ten thousand times more glorious than any which the apostles of old have attained, and if they, one and all, should, swift as the twinkling of an eye, hesitate to recognize the light of My Revelation, their faith shall be of no avail and they shall be accounted among the infidels." " So tremendous is the outpouring of Divine grace in this Dispensation that if mortal hands could be swift enough to record them, within the space of a single day and night there would stream verses of such number as to be equivalent to the whole of the Persian Bayán."*

" *Give heed to my warning, ye people of Persia,*" He thus addresses His countrymen, " *If I be slain at your hands, God will assuredly raise up one who will fill the seat made vacant through my death ; for such is God's method carried into effect of old, and no change can ye find in God's mode of dealing.*" " *Should they attempt to conceal His light on the continent, He will assuredly rear His head in the midmost heart of the ocean and, raising His voice, proclaim : ' I am the lifegiver of the world ! ' . . . And if they cast Him into a darksome pit, they will find Him seated on earth's loftiest heights calling aloud to all mankind : ' Lo, the Desire of the world is come in His majesty, His sovereignty, His transcendent dominion ! ' And if He be buried beneath the depths of the earth, His spirit soaring to the apex of heaven shall peal the summons : ' Behold ye the coming of the Glory ; witness ye the Kingdom of God, the most Holy, the Gracious, the All-Powerful ! ' "* " *Within the throat of this Youth,*" is yet another astounding statement, " *there lie prisoned accents which, if revealed to mankind to an extent smaller than a needle's eye, would suffice to cause every mountain to crumble, the leaves of the trees to be discoloured and their fruits to fall ; would compel every head to bow down in worship and every face to turn in adoration towards this omnipotent Ruler Who, at sundry times and in diverse manners, appeareth as a devouring flame, as a billowing ocean, as a radiant light, as the tree which, rooted in the soil of holiness, lifteth its branches and spreadeth out its limbs as far as and beyond the throne of deathless glory.*"

Anticipating the System which the irresistible power of His Law was destined to unfold in a later age, He writes : " *The world's equilibrium hath been upset through the vibrating influence of this most great, this new World Order. Mankind's ordered life hath been revolutionized through the agency of this unique, this wondrous System — the like of which mortal eyes have never witnessed."* " *The Hand of Omnipotence hath established His Revelation upon an unassailable, an enduring foundation. Storms of human strife are powerless to undermine its basis, nor will men's fanciful theories succeed in damaging its structure."*

In the Súratu'l-Haykal, one of the most challenging works of Bahá'u'lláh, the following verses, each of which testifies to the resistless power infused into the Revelation proclaimed by its Author, have been recorded : " *Naught is seen in My temple but the Temple of God, and in My beauty but His Beauty, and in My being but His Being, and in My self but His Self, and in My movement but His Movement, and in My acquiescence but His Acquiescence, and in My pen but His Pen, the Mighty, the All-Praised. There hath not been in My soul but the Truth, and in Myself naught could be seen but God."* " *The Holy Spirit Itself hath been generated through the agency of a single letter revealed by this Most Great Spirit, if ye be of them that comprehend."* . . . " *Within the treasury of Our Wisdom there lies unrevealed a knowledge, one word of which, if we chose to divulge it to mankind, would cause every human being to recognize the Manifestation of God and to acknowledge His omniscience, would enable every one to discover the secrets of all the sciences, and to attain so high a station as to find himself wholly independent of all past and future learning. Other knowledges We do as well possess, not a single letter of which We can disclose, nor do We find humanity able to hear even the barest reference to their meaning. Thus have We informed you of the knowledge of God, the All-Knowing, the All-Wise."* " *The day is approaching when God will have, by an act of His Will, raised up a race of men the nature of which is inscrutable to all save God, the All-Powerful, the Self-Subsisting."* " *He will, ere long, out of the Bosom of Power draw forth the Hands of Ascendency and Might — Hands who will arise to win victory for this Youth and who will purge mankind from the defilement of the outcast and the ungodly. These Hands will gird up their loins to champion the Faith of God, and will, in*

My name the self-subsistent, the mighty, subdue the peoples and kindreds of the earth. They will enter the cities and will inspire with fear the hearts of all their inhabitants. Such are the evidences of the might of God ; how fearful, how vehement is His might ! "

Such is, dearly-beloved friends, Bahá'u'lláh's own written testimony to the nature of His Revelation. To the affirmations of the Báb, each of which reinforces the strength, and confirms the truth, of these remarkable statements, I have already referred. What remains for me to consider in this connection are such passages in the writings of 'Abdu'l-Bahá, the appointed Interpreter of these same utterances, as throw further light upon and amplify various features of this enthralling theme. The tone of His language is indeed as emphatic and His tribute no less glowing than that of either Bahá'u'lláh or the Báb.

" *Centuries, nay ages, must pass away,*" He affirms in one of His earliest Tablets, " *ere the Day-Star of Truth shineth again in its mid-summer splendour, or appeareth once more in the radiance of its vernal glory . . . How thankful must we be for having been made in this Day the recipients of so overwhelming a favour ! Would that we had ten thousand lives that we might lay them down in thanksgiving for so rare a privilege, so high an attainment, so priceless a bounty !* " " *The mere contemplation,*" He adds, " *of the Dispensation inaugurated by the Blessed Beauty would have sufficed to overwhelm the saints of bygone ages — saints who longed to partake for one moment of its great glory.*" " *The holy ones of past ages and centuries have, each and all, yearned with tearful eyes to live, though for one moment, in the Day of God. Their longings unsatisfied, they repaired to the Great Beyond. How great, therefore, is the bounty of the Abhá Beauty Who, notwithstanding our utter unworthiness, hath through His grace and mercy breathed into us in this divinely-illumined century the spirit of life, hath gathered us beneath the standard of the Beloved of the world, and chosen to confer upon us a bounty for which the mighty ones of bygone ages had craved in vain.*" " *The souls of the well-favoured among the concourse on high,*" He likewise affirms, " *the sacred dwellers of the most exalted Paradise, are in this day filled with burning desire to return unto*

*this world, that they may render such service as lieth in their power
to the threshold of the Abhá Beauty."*

" *The effulgence of God's splendrous mercy,*" He, in a passage
alluding to the growth and future development of the Faith,
declares, " *hath enveloped the peoples and kindreds of the earth, and
the whole world is bathed in its shining glory . . . The day will
soon come when the light of Divine unity will have so permeated
the East and the West that no man dare any longer ignore it.*" " *Now
in the world of being the Hand of divine power hath firmly laid the
foundations of this all-highest bounty and this wondrous gift. Whatsoever is latent in the innermost of this holy cycle shall gradually
appear and be made manifest, for now is but the beginning of its
growth and the day-spring of the revelation of its signs. Ere the
close of this century and of this age, it shall be made clear and evident
how wondrous was that springtide and how heavenly was that gift !* "

In confirmation of the exalted rank of the true believer, referred
to by Bahá'u'lláh, He reveals the following : " *The station which he
who hath truly recognized this Revelation will attain is the same as
the one ordained for such prophets of the house of Israel as are not
regarded as Manifestations ' endowed with constancy.'* "

In connection with the Manifestations destined to follow the
Revelation of Bahá'u'lláh, 'Abdu'l-Bahá makes this definite and
weighty declaration : " *Concerning the Manifestations that will
come down in the future ' in the shadows of the clouds,' know verily that
in so far as their relation to the source of their inspiration is concerned
they are under the shadow of the Ancient Beauty. In their relation,
however, to the age in which they appear, each and every one of them
' doeth whatsoever He willeth.'* "

" *O my friend !* " He thus addresses in one of His Tablets a
man of recognized authority and standing, " *The undying Fire which
the Lord of the Kingdom hath kindled in the midst of the holy Tree
is burning fiercely in the midmost heart of the world. The conflagra-
tion it will provoke will envelop the whole earth. Its blazing flames
will illuminate its peoples and kindreds. All the signs have been
revealed ; every prophetic allusion hath been manifested. Whatever*

*hath been enshrined in all the Scriptures of the past hath been made
evident.   To doubt or hesitate is no more possible . . .   Time is
pressing.   The Divine Charger is impatient, and can tarry no longer.
Ours is the duty to rush forward and, ere it is too late, win the
victory.*" And finally, is this most stirring passage which He, in one
of His moments of exultation, was moved to address to one of His
most trusted and eminent followers in the earliest days of His
ministry : " *What more shall I say ?   What else can my pen recount ?
So loud is the call that reverberates from the Abhá Kingdom that
mortal ears are well-nigh deafened with its vibrations.   The whole
creation, methinks, is being disrupted and is bursting asunder through
the shattering influence of the Divine summons issued from the throne
of glory.   More than this I cannot write.*"

Dearly-beloved friends !   Enough has been said, and the
quoted excerpts from the writings of the Báb, of Bahá'u'lláh and of
'Abdu'l-Bahá are sufficiently numerous and varied, to convince the
conscientious reader of the sublimity of this unique cycle in the
world's religious history.   It would be utterly impossible to over-
exaggerate its significance or to overrate the influence it has exerted
and which it must increasingly exert as its great system unfolds
itself amidst the welter of a collapsing civilization.

To whoever may read these pages a word of warning seems,
however, advisable before I proceed further with the development
of my argument.   Let no one meditating, in the light of the afore-
quoted passages, on the nature of the Revelation of Bahá'u'lláh,
mistake its character or misconstrue the intent of its Author.   The
divinity attributed to so great a Being and the complete incarnation
of the names and attributes of God in so exalted a Person should,
under no circumstances, be misconceived or misinterpreted.   The
human temple that has been made the vehicle of so overpowering
a Revelation must, if we be faithful to the tenets of our Faith, ever
remain entirely distinguished from that " innermost Spirit of
Spirits " and " eternal Essence of Essences "— that invisible yet
rational God Who, however much we extol the divinity of His
Manifestations on earth, can in no wise incarnate His infinite, His

unknowable, His incorruptible and all-embracing Reality in the concrete and limited frame of a mortal being. Indeed, the God Who could so incarnate His own reality would, in the light of the teachings of Bahá'u'lláh, cease immediately to be God. So crude and fantastic a theory of Divine incarnation is as removed from, and incompatible with, the essentials of Bahá'í belief as are the no less inadmissible pantheistic and anthropomorphic conceptions of God — both of which the utterances of Bahá'u'lláh emphatically repudiate and the fallacy of which they expose.

He Who in unnumbered passages claimed His utterance to be the " *Voice of Divinity, the Call of God Himself* " thus solemnly affirms in the Kitáb-i-Íqán : " *To every discerning and illumined heart it is evident that God, the unknowable Essence, the Divine Being, is immeasurably exalted beyond every human attribute such as corporeal existence, ascent and descent, egress and regress . . . He is, and hath ever been, veiled in the ancient eternity of His Essence, and will remain in His Reality everlastingly hidden from the sight of men . . . He standeth exalted beyond and above all separation and union, all proximity and remoteness . . . 'God was alone; there was none else beside Him' is a sure testimony of this truth.*"

" *From time immemorial,*" Bahá'u'lláh, speaking of God, explains, " *He, the Divine Being, hath been veiled in the ineffable sanctity of His exalted Self, and will everlastingly continue to be wrapt in the inpenetrable mystery of His unknowable Essence . . . Ten thousand Prophets, each a Moses, are thunderstruck upon the Sinai of their search at God's forbidding voice, ' Thou shalt never behold Me ! '; whilst a myriad Messengers, each as great as Jesus, stand dismayed upon their heavenly thrones by the interdiction ' Mine Essence thou shalt never apprehend ! ' " " How bewildering to me, insignificant as I am,*" Bahá'u'lláh in His communion with God affirms, " *is the attempt to fathom the sacred depths of Thy knowledge ! How futile my efforts to visualize the magnitude of the power inherent in Thine handiwork — the revelation of Thy creative power ! " " When I contemplate, O my God, the relationship that bindeth me to Thee,*" He, in yet another prayer revealed in His own handwriting, testifies, " *I am moved to proclaim to all created things ' verily I am God ! '; and when I consider my own self, lo, I find it coarser than clay ! "*

" *The door of the knowledge of the Ancient of Days,*" Bahá'u'lláh further states in the Kitáb-i-Íqán, " *being thus closed in the face of all beings, He, the Source of infinite grace . . . hath caused those luminous Gems of Holiness to appear out of the realm of the spirit, in the noble form of the human temple, and be made manifest unto all men, that they may impart unto the world the mysteries of the unchangeable Being and tell of the subtleties of His imperishable Essence . . . All the Prophets of God, His well-favoured, His holy and chosen Messengers are, without exception, the bearers of His names and the embodiments of His attributes . . . These Tabernacles of Holiness, these primal Mirrors which reflect the Light of unfading glory, are but expressions of Him Who is the Invisible of the Invisibles.*"

That Bahá'u'lláh should, notwithstanding the overwhelming intensity of His Revelation, be regarded as essentially one of these Manifestations of God, never to be identified with that invisible Reality, the Essence of Divinity itself, is one of the major beliefs of our Faith — a belief which should never be obscured and the integrity of which no one of its followers should allow to be compromised.

Nor does the Bahá'í Revelation, claiming as it does to be the culmination of a prophetic cycle and the fulfilment of the promise of all ages, attempt, under any circumstances, to invalidate those first and everlasting principles that animate and underlie the religions that have preceded it. The God-given authority, vested in each one of them, it admits and establishes as its firmest and ultimate basis. It regards them in no other light except as different stages in the eternal history and constant evolution of one religion, Divine and indivisible, of which it itself forms but an integral part. It neither seeks to obscure their Divine origin, nor to dwarf the admitted magnitude of their colossal achievements. It can counte-nance no attempt that seeks to distort their features or to stultify the truths which they instil. Its teachings do not deviate a hairbreadth from the verities they enshrine, nor does the weight of its message detract one jot or one tittle from the influence they exert or the loyalty they inspire. Far from aiming at the overthrow of the spiritual foundation of the world's religious systems, its avowed, its unalterable purpose is to widen their basis, to restate their fundamentals, to reconcile their aims, to reinvigorate their life, to demonstrate their oneness, to restore the pristine purity of their teachings, to co-ordinate their functions and to assist in the realization of their highest aspirations. These divinely-revealed religions, as a close observer has graphically expressed it, " are doomed not to die, but to be reborn . . . ' Does not the child succumb in the youth and the youth in the man ; yet neither child nor youth perishes ? ' "

"*They Who are the Luminaries of Truth and the Mirrors reflecting the light of Divine Unity,*" Bahá'u'lláh explains in the Kitáb-i-Íqán, " *in whatever age and cycle they are sent down from their invisible habitations of ancient glory unto this world to educate the souls of men and endue with grace all created things, are invariably endowed with an all-compelling power and invested with invincible sovereignty . . . These sanctified Mirrors, these Day-springs of ancient glory are one and all the exponents on earth of Him Who is the central Orb of the universe, its essence and ultimate purpose. From Him proceed their knowledge and power ; from Him is derived their sovereignty. The beauty of their countenance is but a reflection of His image, and their revelation a sign of His deathless glory . . . Through them is transmitted a grace that is infinite, and by them is revealed the light that can never fade . . . Human tongue can never befittingly sing their praise, and human speech can never unfold their mystery.*" " *Inasmuch as these Birds of the celestial Throne,*" He adds, " *are all sent down from the heaven of the Will of God, and as they all arise to proclaim His irresistible Faith, they therefore are regarded as one soul and the same person . . . They all abide in the same tabernacle, soar in the same heaven, are seated upon the same throne, utter the same speech, and proclaim the same Faith . . . They only differ in the intensity of their revelation and the comparative potency of their light . . . That a certain attribute of God hath not been outwardly manifested by these Essences of Detachment doth in no wise imply that they Who are the Daysprings of God's attributes and the Treasuries of His holy names did not actually possess it.*"

It should also be borne in mind that, great as is the power manifested by this Revelation and however vast the range of the Dispensation its Author has inaugurated, it emphatically repudiates the claim to be regarded as the final revelation of God's will and purpose for mankind. To hold such a conception of its character and functions would be tantamount to a betrayal of its cause and a denial of its truth. It must necessarily conflict with the fundamental principle which constitutes the bedrock of Bahá'í belief, the principle that religious truth is not absolute but relative, that Divine Revelation is orderly, continuous and progressive and not spasmodic or final. Indeed, the categorical rejection by the followers of the Faith of Bahá'u'lláh of the claim to finality which any religious system inaugurated by the Prophets of the past may advance is as clear and emphatic as their own refusal to claim that same finality for the Revelation with which they stand identified. " *To believe that all revelation is ended, that the portals of Divine mercy are closed, that from the day-springs of eternal holiness no sun shall rise again, that the ocean of everlasting bounty is forever stilled, and that out of the tabernacle of ancient glory the Messengers of God have ceased to be made manifest* " must constitute in the eyes of every follower of the Faith a grave, an inexcusable departure from one of its most cherished and fundamental principles.

A reference to some of the already quoted utterances of Bahá'u'lláh and 'Abdu'l-Bahá will surely suffice to establish, beyond the shadow of a doubt, the truth of this cardinal principle. Might not the following passage of the Hidden Words be, likewise, construed as an allegorical allusion to the progressiveness of Divine Revelation and an admission by its Author that the Message with which He has been entrusted is not the final and ultimate expression of the will and guidance of the Almighty ? " *O Son of Justice ! In the night-season the beauty of the immortal Being hath repaired from the emerald height of fidelity unto the Sadratu'l-Muntahá, and wept with such a weeping that the concourse on high and the dwellers of the realms above wailed at His lamenting. Whereupon there was asked, Why the wailing and weeping? He made reply: As bidden I waited expectant upon the hill of faithfulness, yet inhaled not from them that dwell on earth the frangrance of fidelity. Then summoned to return I beheld, and lo! certain doves of holiness were sore tried within the claws of the dogs of earth. Thereupon the Maid of heaven hastened forth unveiled and resplendent from Her mystic mansion, and asked of their names, and all were told but one. And when urged, the first letter thereof was uttered, whereupon the dwellers of the celestial chambers rushed forth out of their habitation of glory. And whilst the second letter was pronounced they fell down, one and all, upon the dust. At that moment a voice was heard from the inmost shrine: ' Thus far and no farther.' Verily We bear witness to that which they have done and now are doing."*

In a more explicit language Bahá'u'lláh testifies to this truth in one of His Tablets revealed in Adrianople: " *Know verily that the veil hiding Our countenance hath not been completely lifted. We have revealed Our Self to a degree corresponding to the capacity of the people of Our age. Should the Ancient Beauty be unveiled in the fulness of His glory mortal eyes would be blinded by the dazzling intensity of His revelation.*"

In the Súriy-i-Ṣabr, revealed as far back as the year 1863, on the very first day of His arrival in the garden of Riḍván, He thus affirms: " *God hath sent down His Messengers to succeed to Moses and Jesus, and He will continue to do so till ' the end that hath no end' ; so that His grace may, from the heaven of Divine bounty, be continually vouchsafed to mankind.*"

" *I am not apprehensive for My own self,*" Bahá'u'lláh still more explicitly declares, " *My fears are for Him Who will be sent down unto you after Me — Him Who will be invested with great sovereignty and mighty dominion.*" And again He writes in the Súratu'l-Haykal: " *By those words which I have revealed, Myself is not intended, but rather He Who will come after Me. To it is witness God, the All-Knowing.*" " *Deal not with Him,*" He adds, "*as ye have dealt with Me.*"

In a more circumstantial passage the Báb upholds the same truth in His writings. " *It is clear and evident*," He writes in the Persian Bayán, " *that the object of all preceding Dispensations hath been to pave the way for the advent of Muḥammad, the Apostle of God. These, including the Muḥammadan Dispensation, have had, in their turn, as their objective the Revelation proclaimed by the Qá'im. The purpose underlying this Revelation, as well as those that preceded it, has, in like manner, been to announce the advent of the Faith of Him Whom God will make manifest. And this Faith — the Faith of Him Whom God will make manifest — in its turn, together with all the Revelations gone before it, have as their object the Manifestation destined to succeed it. And the latter, no less than all the Revelations preceding it, prepare the way for the Revelation which is yet to follow. The process of the rise and setting of the Sun of Truth will thus indefinitely continue — a process that hath had no beginning and will have no end.*"

" *Know of a certainty,*" Bahá'u'lláh explains in this connection, " *that in every Dispensation the light of Divine Revelation has been vouchsafed to men in direct proportion to their spiritual capacity. Consider the sun. How feeble its rays the moment it appeareth above the horizon. How gradually its warmth and potency increase as it approacheth its zenith, enabling meanwhile all created things to adapt themselves to the growing intensity of its light. How steadily it declines until it reacheth its setting point. Were it all of a sudden to manifest the energies latent within it, it would no doubt cause injury to all created things . . In like manner, if the Sun of Truth were suddenly to reveal, at the earliest stages of its manifestation, the full measure of the potencies which the providence of the Almighty hath bestowed upon it, the earth of human understanding would waste away and be consumed; for men's hearts would neither sustain the intensity of its revelation, nor be able to mirror forth the radiance of its light. Dismayed and overpowered, they would cease to exist.*"

In the light of these clear and conclusive statements it is our clear duty to make it indubitably evident to every seeker after truth that from " the beginning that hath no beginning " the Prophets of the one, the unknowable God, including Bahá'u'lláh Himself, have all, as the channels of God's grace, as the exponents of His unity, as the mirrors of His light and the revealers of His purpose, been commissioned to unfold to mankind an ever-increasing measure of His truth, of His inscrutable will and Divine guidance, and will continue to " the end that hath no end " to vouchsafe still fuller and mightier revelations of His limitless power and glory.

We might well ponder in our hearts the following passages from a prayer revealed by Bahá'u'lláh which strikingly affirm, and are a further evidence of, the reality of the great and essential truth lying at the very core of His Message to mankind : " *Praise be to Thee, O Lord my God, for the wondrous revelations of Thine inscrutable decree and the manifold woes and trials Thou hast destined for myself. At one time Thou didst deliver me into the hands of Nimrod ; at another Thou hast allowed Pharaoh's rod to persecute me. Thou alone canst estimate, through Thy all-encompassing knowledge and the operation of Thy Will, the incalculable afflictions I have suffered at their hands. Again Thou didst cast me into the prison-cell of the ungodly for no reason except that I was moved to whisper into the ears of the well-favoured denizens of Thy kingdom an intimation of the vision with which Thou hadst, through Thy knowledge, inspired me and revealed to me its meaning through the potency of Thy might. And again Thou didst decree that I be beheaded by the sword of the infidel. Again I was crucified for having unveiled to men's eyes the hidden gems of Thy glorious unity, for having revealed to them the wondrous signs of Thy sovereign and everlasting power. How bitter the humiliations heaped upon me, in a subsequent age, on the plain of Karbilá ! How lonely did I feel amidst Thy people ; to what state of helplessness I was reduced in that land ! Unsatisfied with such indignities, my persecutors decapitated me and carrying aloft my head from land to land paraded it before the gaze of the unbelieving multitude and deposited it on the seats of the perverse and faithless. In a later age I was suspended and my breast was made a target to the darts of the malicious cruelty of my foes. My limbs were riddled with bullets and my body was torn asunder. Finally, behold how in this day my treacherous enemies have leagued themselves against me, and are continually plotting to instil the venom of hate and malice into the souls of Thy servants. With all their might they are scheming to accomplish their purpose . . . Grievous as is my plight, O God, my Well-beloved, I render thanks unto Thee, and my spirit is grateful for whatsoever hath befallen me in the path of Thy good-pleasure. I am well pleased with that which Thou didst ordain for me, and welcome, however calamitous, the pains and sorrows I am made to suffer."*

THE BÁB

Dearly-beloved friends ! That the Báb, the inaugurator of the Bábí Dispensation, is fully entitled to rank as one of the self-sufficient Manifestations of God, that He has been invested with sovereign power and authority, and exercises all the rights and prerogatives of independent Prophethood, is yet another fundamental verity which the Message of Bahá'u'lláh insistently proclaims and which its followers must uncompromisingly uphold. That He is not to be regarded merely as an inspired Precursor of the Bahá'í Revelation, that in His person, as He Himself bears witness in the Persian Bayán, the object of all the Prophets gone before Him has been fulfilled, is a truth which I feel it my duty to demonstrate and emphasize. We would assuredly be failing in our duty to the Faith we profess and would be violating one of its basic and sacred principles if in our words or by our conduct we hesitate to recognise the implications of this root principle of Bahá'í belief, or refuse to uphold unreservedly its integrity and demonstrate its truth. Indeed the chief motive actuating me to undertake the task of editing and translating Nabíl's immortal Narrative has been to enable every follower of the Faith in the West to better understand and more readily grasp the tremendous implications of His exalted station and to more ardently admire and love Him.

There can be no doubt that the claim to the twofold station ordained for the Báb by the Almighty, a claim which He Himself has so boldly advanced, which Bahá'u'lláh has repeatedly affirmed, and to which the Will and Testament of 'Abdu'l-Bahá has finally given the sanction of its testimony, constitutes the most distinctive feature of the Bahá'í Dispensation. It is a further evidence of its uniqueness, a tremendous accession to the strength, to the mysterious power and authority with which this holy cycle has been invested. Indeed the greatness of the Báb consists primarily, not in His being the divinely-appointed Forerunner of so transcendent a Revelation, but rather in His having been invested with the powers inherent in the inaugurator of a separate religious Dispensation, and in His wielding, to a degree unrivalled by the Messengers gone before Him, the sceptre of independent Prophethood.

The short duration of His Dispensation, the restricted range within which His laws and ordinances have been made to operate, supply no criterion whatever wherewith to judge its Divine origin and to evaluate the potency of its message. " *That so brief a span,*" Bahá'u'lláh Himself explains, " *should have separated this most mighty and wondrous Revelation from Mine own previous Manifestation, is a secret that no man can unravel and a mystery such as no mind can fathom. Its duration had been fore-ordained, and no man shall ever discover its reason unless and until he be informed of the contents of My Hidden Book.*" " *Behold,*" Bahá'u'lláh further explains in the Kitáb-i-Badí', one of His works refuting the arguments of the people of the Bayán, " *behold, how immediately upon the completion of the ninth year of this wondrous, this most holy and merciful Dispensation, the requisite number of pure, of wholly consecrated and sanctified souls had been most secretly consummated.*"

The marvellous happenings that have heralded the advent of the Founder of the Bábí Dispensation, the dramatic circumstances of His own eventful life, the miraculous tragedy of His martyrdom, the magic of His influence exerted on the most eminent and powerful among His countrymen, to all of which every chapter of Nabíl's stirring narrative testifies, should in themselves be regarded as sufficient evidence of the validity of His claim to so exalted a station among the Prophets.

However graphic the record which the eminent chronicler of His life has transmitted to posterity, so luminous a narrative must pale before the glowing tribute paid to the Báb by the pen of Bahá'u'lláh. This tribute the Báb Himself has, by the clear assertion of His claim, abundantly supported, while the written testimonies of 'Abdu'l-Bahá have powerfully reinforced its character and elucidated its meaning.

Where else if not in the Kitáb-i-Íqán can the student of the Bábí Dispensation seek to find those affirmations that unmistakably attest the power and spirit which no man, except he be a Manifestation of God, can manifest? "*Could such a thing,*" exclaims Bahá'u'lláh, "*be made manifest except through the power of a Divine Revelation and the potency of God's invincible Will? By the righteousness of God! Were any one to entertain so great a Revelation in his heart the thought of such a declaration would alone confound him! Were the hearts of all men to be crowded into his heart, he would still hesitate to venture upon so awful an enterprise.*" "*No eye,*" He in another passage affirms, "*hath beheld so great an outpouring of bounty, nor hath any ear heard of such a Revelation of loving-kindness . . . The Prophets ' endowed with constancy,' whose loftiness and glory shine as the sun, were each honoured with a Book which all have seen, and the verses of which have been duly ascertained. Whereas the verses which have rained from this Cloud of divine mercy have been so abundant that none hath yet been able to estimate their number . . . How can they belittle this Revelation? Hath any age witnessed such momentous happenings?*"

Commenting on the character and influence of those heroes and martyrs whom the spirit of the Báb had so magically transformed Bahá'u'lláh reveals the following: "*If these companions be not the true strivers after God, who else could be called by this name? . . . If these companions, with all their marvellous testimonies and wondrous works, be false, who then is worthy to claim for himself the truth? . . . Has the world since the days of Adam witnessed such tumult, such violent commotion? . . . Methinks, patience was revealed only by virtue of their fortitude, and faithfulness itself was begotten only by their deeds.*"

Wishing to stress the sublimity of the Báb's exalted station as compared with that of the Prophets of the past, Bahá'u'lláh in that same epistle asserts: "*No understanding can grasp the nature of His Revelation, nor can any knowledge comprehend the full measure of His Faith.*" He then quotes, in confirmation of His argument, these prophetic words: "*Knowledge is twenty and seven letters. All that the Prophets have revealed are two letters thereof. No man thus far hath known more than these two letters. But when the Qá'im shall arise, He will cause the remaining twenty and five letters to be made manifest.*" "*Behold,*" He adds, "*how great and lofty is His station ! His rank excelleth that of all the Prophets and His Revelation transcendeth the comprehension and understanding of all their chosen ones." " Of His Revelation," He further adds, " the Prophets of God, His saints and chosen ones, have either not been informed, or, in pursuance of God's inscrutable decree, they have not disclosed."*

Of all the tributes which Bahá'u'lláh's unerring pen has chosen to pay to the memory of the Báb, His " Best-Beloved," the most memorable and touching is this brief, yet eloquent passage which so greatly enhances the value of the concluding passages of that same epistle. " *Amidst them all,*" He writes, referring to the afflictive trials and dangers besetting Him in the city of Baghdád, "*We stand life in hand wholly resigned to His Will, that perchance through God's loving kindness and grace, this revealed and manifest Letter* (Bahá'u'lláh) *may lay down His life as a sacrifice in the path of the Primal Point, the most exalted Word* (the Báb). *By Him, at Whose bidding the Spirit hath spoken, but for this yearning of Our soul, We would not, for one moment, have tarried any longer in this city.*"

Dearly-beloved friends ! So resounding a praise, so bold an assertion issued by the pen of Bahá'u'lláh in so weighty a work, are fully re-echoed in the language in which the Source of the Bábí Revelation has chosen to clothe the claims He Himself has advanced. " *I am the Mystic Fane,*" the Báb thus proclaims His station in the Qayyúmu'l-Asmá', " *which the Hand of Omnipotence hath reared. I am the Lamp which the Finger of God hath lit within its niche and caused to shine with deathless splendour. I am the Flame of that supernal Light that glowed upon Sinai in the gladsome Spot, and lay concealed in the midst of the Burning Bush.*" " *O Qurratu'l-'Ayn !* " He, addressing Himself in that same commentary, exclaims, " *I recognize in Thee none other except the ' Great Announcement '— the Announcement voiced by the Concourse on high. By this name, I bear witness, they that circle the Throne of Glory have ever known Thee.*" " *With each and every Prophet, Whom We have sent down in the past,*" He further adds, " *We have established a separate Covenant concerning the ' Remembrance of God ' and His Day. Manifest, in the realm of glory and through the power of truth, are the ' Remembrance of God ' and His Day before the eyes of the*

angels that circle His mercy-seat."   " Should it be Our wish," He
again affirms, *" it is in Our power to compel, through the agency of
but one letter of Our Revelation, the world and all that is therein to
recognize, in less than the twinkling of an eye, the truth of Our Cause."*

" *I am the Primal Point,"* the Báb thus addresses Muḥammad
S͟háh from the prison-fortress of Máh-Kú, *" from which have been
generated all created things . . . I am the Countenance of God
Whose splendour can never be obscured, the light of God whose
radiance can never fade . . . All the keys of heaven God hath chosen
to place on My right hand, and all the keys of hell on My left . . .
I am one of the sustaining pillars of the Primal Word of God. Whosoever hath recognized Me, hath known all that is true and right,
and hath attained all that is good and seemly . . . The substance
wherewith God hath created Me is not the clay out of which others
have been formed. He hath conferred upon Me that which the
worldly-wise can never comprehend, nor the faithful discover."*
" *Should a tiny ant,"* the Báb, wishing to stress the limitless
potentialities latent in His Dispensation, characteristically affirms,
" *desire in this day to be possessed of such power as to be able to unravel
the abstrusest and most bewildering passages of the Qur'án, its wish
will no doubt be fulfilled, inasmuch as the mystery of eternal might
vibrates within the innermost being of all created things."   " If so
helpless a creature,"* is 'Abdu'l-Bahá's comment on so startling
an affirmation, " *can be endowed with so subtle a capacity, how much
more efficacious must be the power released through the liberal effusions
of the grace of Bahá'u'lláh ! "*

To these authoritative assertions and solemn declarations made
by Bahá'u'lláh and the Báb must be added 'Abdu'l-Bahá's own
incontrovertible testimony. He, the appointed interpreter of the
utterances of both Bahá'u'lláh and the Báb, corroborates, not by
implication but in clear and categorical language, both in His
Tablets and in His Testament, the truth of the statements to which
I have already referred.

In a Tablet addressed to a Bahá'í in Mázindarán, in which He
unfolds the meaning of a misinterpreted statement attributed to
Him regarding the rise of the Sun of Truth in this century, He

sets forth, briefly but conclusively, what should remain for all time our true conception of the relationship between the two Manifestations associated with the Bahá'í Dispensation. " *In making such a statement,*" He explains, " *I had in mind no one else except the Báb and Bahá'u'lláh, the character of Whose Revelations it had been my purpose to elucidate. The Revelation of the Báb may be likened to the sun, its station corresponding to the first sign of the Zodiac — the sign Aries — which the sun enters at the Vernal Equinox. The station of Bahá'u'lláh's Revelation, on the other hand, is represented by the sign Leo, the sun's mid-summer and highest station. By this is meant that this holy Dispensation is illumined with the light of the Sun of Truth shining from its most exalted station, and in the plenitude of its resplendency, its heat and glory.*"

" *The Báb, the Exalted One,*" 'Abdu'l-Bahá more specifically affirms in another Tablet, " *is the Morn of Truth, the splendour of Whose light shineth throughout all regions. He is also the Harbinger of the Most Great Light, the Abhá Luminary. The Blessed Beauty is the One promised by the sacred books of the past, the revelation of the Source of light that shone upon Mount Sinai, Whose fire glowed in the midst of the Burning Bush. We are, one and all, servants of their threshold, and stand each as a lowly keeper at their door.*" " *Every proof and prophecy,*" is His still more emphatic warning, " *every manner of evidence, whether based on reason or on the text of the scriptures and traditions, are to be regarded as centred in the persons of Bahá'u'lláh and the Báb. In them is to be found their complete fulfilment.*"

And finally, in His Will and Testament, the repository of His last wishes and parting instructions, He in the following passage, specifically designed to set forth the guiding principles of Bahá'í belief, sets the seal of His testimony on the Báb's dual and exalted station : " *The foundation of the belief of the people of Bahá (may my life be offered up for them) is this : His holiness the exalted One* (the Báb) *is the Manifestation of the unity and oneness of God and the Forerunner of the Ancient Beauty* (Bahá'u'lláh). *His holiness, the Abhá Beauty* (Bahá'u'lláh) (*may my life be offered up as a sacrifice for His steadfast friends*) *is the supreme Manifestation of God and the Dayspring of His most divine Essence.*" " *All others,*" He significantly adds, " *are servants unto Him and do His bidding.*"

‘ABDU’L-BAHÁ

Dearly-beloved friends ! I have in the foregoing pages ventured to attempt an exposition of such truths as I firmly believe are implicit in the claim of Him Who is the Fountain-Head of the Bahá'í Revelation. I have moreover endeavoured to dissipate such misapprehensions as may naturally arise in the mind of any one contemplating so superhuman a manifestation of the glory of God. I have striven to explain the meaning of the divinity with which He Who is the vehicle of so mysterious an energy must needs be invested. That the Message which so great a Being has, in this age, been commissioned by God to deliver to mankind recognizes the divine origin and upholds the first principles of every Dispensation inaugurated by the prophets of the past, and stands inextricably interwoven with each one of them, I have also to the best of my ability undertaken to demonstrate. That the Author of such a Faith, Who repudiates the claim to finality which leaders of various denominations uphold has, despite the vastness of His Revelation, disclaimed it for Himself I have, likewise, felt it necessary to prove and emphasize. That the Báb, notwithstanding the duration of His Dispensation, should be regarded primarily, not as the chosen Precursor of the Bahá'í Faith, but as One invested with the un-divided authority assumed by each of the independent Prophets of the past, seemed to me yet another basic principle the elucidation of which would be extremely desirable at the present stage of the evolution of our Cause.

An attempt I strongly feel should now be made to clarify our minds regarding the station occupied by 'Abdu'l-Bahá and the significance of His position in this holy Dispensation. It would be indeed difficult for us, who stand so close to such a tremendous figure and are drawn by the mysterious power of so magnetic a personality, to obtain a clear and exact understanding of the role and character of One Who, not only in the Dispensation of Bahá'u'-lláh but in the entire field of religious history, fulfils a unique func-tion. Though moving in a sphere of His own and holding a rank radically different from that of the Author and the Forerunner of the Bahá'í Revelation, He, by virtue of the station ordained for Him through the Covenant of Bahá'u'lláh, forms together with them what may be termed the Three Central Figures of a Faith that stands unapproached in the world's spiritual history. He towers, in conjunction with them, above the destinies of this infant Faith of God from a level to which no individual or body minister- ing to its needs after Him, and for no less a period than a full thousand years, can ever hope to rise. To degrade His lofty rank by identifying His station with or by regarding it as roughly equivalent to, the position of those on whom the mantle of His authority has fallen would be an act of impiety as grave as the no less heretical belief that inclines to exalt Him to a state of absolute equality with either the central Figure or Forerunner of our Faith. For wide as is the gulf that separates 'Abdu'l-Bahá from Him Who is the Source of an independent Revelation, it can never be regarded as commensurate with the greater distance that stands between Him Who is the Centre of the Covenant and His ministers who are to carry on His work, whatever be their name, their rank, their func- tions or their future achievements. Let those who have known 'Abdu'l-Bahá, who through their contact with His magnetic personality have come to cherish for Him so fervent an admiration, reflect, in the light of this statement, on the greatness of One Who is so far above Him in station.

That 'Abdu'l-Bahá is not a Manifestation of God, that, though the successor of His Father, He does not occupy a cognate station, that no one else except the Báb and Bahá'u'lláh can ever lay claim to such a station before the expiration of a full thousand years — are verities which lie embedded in the specific utterances of both the Founder of our Faith and the Interpreter of His teachings.

" *Whoso layeth claim to a Revelation direct from God,*" is the express warning uttered in the Kitáb-i-Aqdas, " *ere the expiration of a full thousand years, such a man is assuredly a lying impostor. We pray God that He may graciously assist him to retract and repudi- ate such claim. Should he repent, God will no doubt forgive him. If, however, he persists in his error, God will assuredly send down one who will deal mercilessly with him. Terrible indeed is God in punish-ing !* " " *Whosoever,*" He adds as a further emphasis, " *interpret-eth this verse otherwise than its obvious meaning is deprived of the Spirit of God and of His mercy which encompasseth all created things.*" " *Should a man appear,*" is yet another conclusive state-ment, " *ere the lapse of a full thousand years — each year consisting of twelve months according to the Qur'án, and of nineteen months of nineteen days each, according to the Bayán — and if such a man reveal to your eyes all the signs of God, unhesitatingly reject him !* "

'Abdu'l-Bahá's own statements, in confirmation of this warning, are no less emphatic and binding : " *This is,*" He declares, " *my firm, my unshakable conviction, the essence of my unconcealed and explicit belief — a conviction and belief which the denizens of the Abhá Kingdom fully share : The Blessed Beauty is the Sun of Truth, and His light the light of truth. The Báb is likewise the Sun of Truth, and His light the light of truth . . . My station is the station of servitude — a servitude which is complete, pure and real, firmly established, enduring, obvious, explicitly revealed and subject to no interpretation whatever . . . I am the Interpreter of the Word of God ; such is my interpretation.*"

Does not 'Abdu'l-Bahá in His own Will — in a tone and language that might well confound the most inveterate among the breakers of His Father's Covenant — rob of their chief weapon those who so long and so persistently had striven to impute to Him the charge of having tacitly claimed a station equal, if not superior, to that of Bahá'u'lláh ? " *The foundation of the belief of the people of Bahá is this,*" thus proclaims one of the weightiest passages of that last document left to voice in perpetuity the directions and wishes of a departed Master, " *His Holiness the Exalted One* (the Báb) *is the Manifestation of the unity and oneness of God and the Forerunner of the Ancient Beauty. His Holiness the Abhá Beauty* (Bahá'u'lláh) *(may my life be a sacrifice for His steadfast friends) is the supreme Manifestation of God and the Dayspring of His most divine Essence. All others are servants unto Him and do His bidding.*"

From such clear and formally laid down statements, incompat-ible as they are with any assertion of a claim to Prophethood, we should not by any means infer that 'Abdu'l-Bahá is merely one of the servants of the Blessed Beauty, or at best one whose function is to be confined to that of an authorized interpreter of His Father's teachings. Far be it from me to entertain such a notion or to wish to instil such sentiments. To regard Him in such a light is a manifest betrayal of the priceless heritage bequeathed by Bahá'u'lláh to mankind. Immeasurably exalted is the station conferred upon Him by the supreme Pen above and beyond the implications of these, His own written statements. Whether in the Kitáb-i-Aqdas, the most weighty and sacred of all the works of Bahá'u'lláh, or in the Kitáb-i-'Ahd, the Book of His Covenant, or in the Súriy-i-Ghuṣn (Tablet of the Branch), such references as have been recorded by the pen of Bahá'u'lláh — references which the Tablets of His Father addressed to Him mightily reinforce — invest 'Abdu'l-Bahá with a power, and surround Him with a halo, which the present generation can never adequately appreciate.

He is, and should for all time be regarded, first and foremost, as the Centre and Pivot of Bahá'u'lláh's peerless and all-enfolding Covenant, His most exalted handiwork, the stainless Mirror of His light, the perfect Exemplar of His teachings, the unerring Interpreter of His Word, the embodiment of every Bahá'í ideal, the incarnation of every Bahá'í virtue, the Most Mighty Branch sprung from the Ancient Root, the Limb of the Law of God, the Being "*round Whom all names revolve,*" the Mainspring of the Oneness of Humanity, the Ensign of the Most Great Peace, the Moon of the Central Orb of this most holy Dispensation — styles and titles that are implicit and find their truest, their highest and fairest expression in the magic name 'Abdu'l-Bahá. He is, above and beyond these appellations, the "Mystery of God"— an expression which Bahá'u'lláh Himself has chosen to designate Him, and which, while it does not by any means justify us to assign to Him the station of Prophethood, indicates how in the person of 'Abdu'l-Bahá the incompatible characteristics of a human nature and superhuman knowledge and perfection have been blended and are completely harmonized.

"*When the ocean of My presence hath ebbed and the Book of*

My Revelation is ended," proclaims the Kitáb-i-Aqdas, " *turn your faces towards Him Whom God hath purposed, Who hath branched from this Ancient Root.*" And again, " *When the Mystic Dove will have winged its flight from its Sanctuary of Praise and sought its far-off goal, its hidden habitation, refer ye whatsoever ye understand not in the Book to Him Who hath branched from this mighty Stock.*"

In the Kitáb-i-'Ahd, moreover, Bahá'u'lláh solemnly and explicitly declares : " *It is incumbent upon the Aghsán, the Afnán and My kindred to turn, one and all, their faces towards the Most Mighty Branch. Consider that which We have revealed in Our Most Holy Book : ' When the ocean of My presence hath ebbed and the Book of My Revelation is ended, turn your faces toward Him Whom God hath purposed, Who hath branched from this Ancient Root.' The object of this sacred verse is none other except the Most Mighty Branch* ('Abdu'l-Bahá). *Thus have We graciously revealed unto you our potent Will, and I am verily the Gracious, the All-Powerful.*"

In the Súriy-i-Ghusn (Tablet of the Branch) the following verses have been recorded : " *There hath branched from the Sadratu'l-Muntahá this sacred and glorious Being, this Branch of Holiness ; well is it with him that hath sought His shelter and abideth beneath His shadow. Verily the Limb of the Law of God hath sprung forth from this Root which God hath firmly implanted in the Ground of His Will, and Whose Branch hath been so uplifted as to encompass the whole of creation. Magnified be He, therefore, for this sublime, this blessed, this mighty, this exalted Handiwork ! . . . A Word hath, as a token of Our grace, gone forth from the Most Great Tablet — a Word which God hath adorned with the ornament of His own Self, and made it sovereign over the earth and all that is therein, and a sign of His greatness and power among its people . . . . Render thanks unto God, O people, for His appearance ; for verily He is the most great Favour unto you, the most perfect bounty upon you ; and through Him every mouldering bone is quickened. Whoso turneth towards Him hath turned towards God, and whoso turneth away from Him hath turned away from My Beauty, hath repudiated My Proof, and transgressed against Me. He is the Trust of God amongst you, His charge within you, His manifestation unto*

*you and His appearance among His favoured servants . . . We have
sent Him down in the form of a human temple. Blest and sanctified
be God Who createth whatsoever He willeth through His inviolable,
His infallible decree. They who deprive themselves of the shadow
of the Branch, are lost in the wilderness of error, are consumed by the
heat of worldly desires, and are of those who will assuredly perish."*

" *O Thou Who art the apple of Mine eye !* " Bahá'u'lláh, in His
own handwriting, thus addresses 'Abdu'l-Bahá, " *My glory, the
ocean of My loving-kindness, the sun of My bounty, the heaven of
My mercy rest upon Thee. We pray God to illumine the world
through Thy knowledge and wisdom, to ordain for Thee that which
will gladden Thine heart and impart consolation to Thine eyes."*
" *The glory of God rest upon Thee,*" He writes in another Tablet,
" *and upon whosoever serveth Thee and circleth around Thee. Woe,
great woe, betide him that opposeth and injureth Thee. Well is it
with him that sweareth fealty to Thee ; the fire of hell torment him
who is Thine enemy."* " *We have made Thee a shelter for all mankind,*" He, in yet another Tablet, affirms, " *a shield unto all who
are in heaven and on earth, a stronghold for whosoever hath believed
in God, the Incomparable, the All-Knowing. God grant that through
Thee He may protect them, may enrich and sustain them, that He
may inspire Thee with that which shall be a well-spring of wealth
unto all created things, an ocean of bounty unto all men, and the
dayspring of mercy unto all peoples."*

" *Thou knowest, O my God,*" Bahá'u'lláh, in a prayer revealed
in 'Abdu'l-Bahá's honour, supplicates, " *that I desire for Him
naught except that which Thou didst desire, and have chosen Him for
no purpose save that which Thou hadst intended for Him. Render
Him victorious, therefore, through Thy hosts of earth and heaven
. . . Ordain, I beseech Thee, by the ardour of My love for Thee and
My yearning to manifest Thy Cause, for Him, as well as for them that
love Him, that which Thou hast destined for Thy Messengers and
the Trustees of Thy Revelation. Verily, Thou art the Almighty, the
All-Powerful."*

In a letter dictated by Bahá'u'lláh and addressed by Mírzá Áqá
Ján, His amanuensis, to 'Abdu'l-Bahá while the latter was on a visit

to Beirut, we read the following : " *Praise be to Him Who hath honoured the Land of Bá* (Beirut) *through the presence of Him round Whom all names revolve. All the atoms of the earth have announced unto all created things that from behind the gate of the Prison-city there hath appeared and above its horizon there hath shone forth the Orb of the beauty of the great, the Most Mighty Branch of God — His ancient and immutable Mystery — proceeding on its way to another land. Sorrow, thereby, hath eveloped this Prison-city, whilst another land rejoiceth . . . Blessed, doubly blessed, is the ground which His footsteps have trodden, the eye that hath been cheered by the beauty of His countenance, the ear that hath been honoured by hearkening to His call, the heart that hath tasted the sweetness of His love, the breast that hath dilated through His remembrance, the pen that hath voiced His praise, the scroll that hath borne the testimony of His writings.*"

'Abdu'l-Bahá, writing in confirmation of the authority conferred upon Him by Bahá'u'lláh, makes the following statement : " *In accordance with the explicit text of the Kitáb-i-Aqdas Bahá'u'lláh hath made the Centre of the Covenant the Interpreter of His Word — a Covenant so firm and mighty that from the beginning of time until the present day no religious Dispensation hath produced its like.*"

Exalted as is the rank of 'Abdu'l-Bahá, and however profuse the praises with which in these sacred Books and Tablets Bahá'u'lláh has glorified His son, so unique a distinction must never be construed as conferring upon its recipient a station identical with, or equivalent to, that of His Father, the Manifestation Himself. To give such an interpretation to any of these quoted passages would at once, and for obvious reasons, bring it into conflict with the no less clear and authentic assertions and warnings to which I have already referred. Indeed, as I have already stated, those who overestimate 'Abdu'l-Bahá's station are just as reprehensible and have done just as much harm as those who underestimate it. And this for no other reason except that by insisting upon an altogether unwarranted inference from Bahá'u'lláh's writings they are inadvertently justifying and continuously furnishing the enemy with proofs for his false accusations and misleading statements.

I feel it necessary, therefore, to state without any equivocation or hesitation that neither in the Kitáb-i-Aqdas nor in the Book of Bahá'u'lláh's Covenant, nor even in the Tablet of the Branch, nor in any other Tablet, whether revealed by Bahá'u'lláh or 'Abdu'l-Bahá, is there any authority whatever for the opinion that inclines to uphold the so-called " mystic unity " of Bahá'u'lláh and 'Abdu'l-Bahá, or to establish the identity of the latter with His Father or with any preceding Manifestation.   This erroneous conception may, in part, be ascribed to an altogether extravagant interpretation of certain terms and passages in the Tablet of the Branch, to the introduction into its English translation of certain words that are either non-existent, misleading, or ambiguous in their connotation. It is, no doubt, chiefly based upon an altogether unjustified inference from the opening passages of a Tablet of Bahá'u'lláh, extracts of which, as reproduced in the " Bahá'í Scriptures," immediately precede, but form no part of, the said Tablet of the Branch.   It should be made clear to every one reading those extracts that by the phrase " the Tongue of the Ancient " no one else is meant but God, and that the term " the Greatest Name " is an obvious reference to Bahá'u'lláh, and that " the Covenant " referred to is not the specific Covenant of which Bahá'u'lláh is the immediate Author and 'Abdu'l-Bahá the Centre but that general Covenant which, as inculcated by the Bahá'í teaching, God Himself invariably establishes with mankind when He inaugurates a new Dispensation.   " The Tongue " that " gives," as stated in those extracts, the " glad-tidings " is none other than the Voice of God referring to Bahá'u'lláh, and not Bahá'u'lláh referring to 'Abdu'l-Bahá.

Moreover, to maintain that the assertion " He is Myself," instead of denoting the mystic unity of God and His Manifestations, as explained in the Kitáb-i-Íqán, establishes the identity of Bahá'u'lláh with 'Abdu'l-Bahá, would constitute a direct violation of the oft-repeated principle of the oneness of God's Manifestations — a principle which the Author of these same extracts is seeking by implication to emphasize.

It would also amount to a reversion to those irrational and superstitious beliefs which have insensibly crept, in the first century of the Christian era, into the teachings of Jesus Christ, and by crystallizing into accepted dogmas have impaired the effectiveness and obscured the purpose of the Christian Faith.

" *I affirm*," is 'Abdu'l-Bahá's own written comment on the Tablet of the Branch, " *that the true meaning, the real significance, the innermost secret of these verses, of these very words, is my own serviiude to the sacred Threshold of the Abhá Beauty, my complete self-effacement, my utter nothingness before Him. This is my res-resplendent crown, my most precious adorning. On this I pride myself in the kingdom of earth and heaven. Therein I glory among the company of the well-favoured!* " " *No one is permitted*," He warns us in the passage which immediately follows, " *to give these verses any other interpretation*." " *I am*," He, in this same connection affirms, " *according to the explicit texts of the Kitáb-i-Aqdas and the Kitáb-i-'Ahd the manifest Interpreter of the Word of God . . . Whoso deviates from my interpretation is a victim of his own fancy*."

Furthermore, the inescapable inference from the belief in the identity of the Author of our Faith with Him Who is the Centre of His Covenant would be to place 'Abdu'l-Bahá in a position superior to that of the Báb, the reverse of which is the fundamental, though not as yet universally recognized, principle of this Revelation. It would also justify the charge with which, all throughout 'Abdu'l-Bahá's ministry, the Covenant-Breakers have striven to poison the minds and pervert the understanding of Bahá'u'lláh's loyal followers.

It would be more correct, and in consonance with the established principles of Bahá'u'lláh and the Báb, if instead of maintaining this fictitious identity with reference to 'Abdu'l-Bahá, we regard the Forerunner and the Founder of our Faith as identical in reality — a truth which the text of the Súriy-i-Haykal unmistakably affirms. " *Had the Primal Point* (the Báb) *been someone else beside Me as ye claim*," is Bahá'u'lláh's explicit statement, " *and had attained My presence, verily He would have never allowed Himself to be separated from Me, but rather We would have had mutual delights with each other in My Days." " He Who now voiceth the Word of God,"* Bahá'u'lláh again affirms, *" is none other except the Primal Point Who hath once again been made manifest." " He is,"* He thus refers to Himself in a Tablet addressed to one of the Letters of the Living, *" the same as the One Who appeared in the year sixty* (1260 A.H.). *This verily is one of His mighty signs." " Who,"* He pleads in the Súriy-i-Damm, *" will arise to secure the triumph of the Primal Beauty* (the Báb) *revealed in the countenance of His succeeding Manifestation ? "* Referring to the Revelation proclaimed by the Báb He conversely characterizes it as *" My own previous Manifestation."*

That 'Abdu'l-Bahá is not a Manifestation of God, that He gets His light, His inspiration and sustenance direct from the Fountainhead of the Bahá'í Revelation ; that He reflects even as a clear and perfect Mirror the rays of Bahá'u'lláh's glory, and does not inherently possess that indefinable yet all-pervading reality the exclusive possession of which is the hallmark of Prophethood ; that His words are not equal in rank, though they possess an equal validity with the utterances of Bahá'u'lláh ; that He is not to be acclaimed as the return of Jesus Christ, the Son Who will come " in the glory of the Father "— these truths find added justification, and are further reinforced, by the following statement of 'Abdu'l-Bahá, addressed to some believers in America, with which I may well conclude this section : *" You have written that there is a difference among the believers concerning the ' Second Coming of Christ.' Gracious God ! Time and again this question hath arisen, and its answer hath emanated in a clear and irrefutable statement from the pen of 'Abdu'l-Bahá, that what is meant in the prophecies by the ' Lord of Hosts ' and the ' Promised Christ ' is the Blessed Perfection* (Bahá'u'lláh) *and His holiness the Exalted One* (the Báb). *My name is 'Abdu'l-Bahá. My qualification is 'Abdu'l-Bahá. My reality is 'Abdu'l-Bahá. My praise is 'Abdu'l-Bahá. Thraldom to the Blessed Perfection is my glorious and refulgent diadem, and servitude to all the human race my perpetual religion . . . No name, no title, no mention, no commendation have I, nor will ever have, except 'Abdu'l-Bahá. This is my longing. This is my greatest yearning. This is my eternal life. This is my everlasting glory."*

THE ADMINISTRATIVE ORDER

Dearly-beloved brethren in 'Abdu'l-Bahá ! With the ascension of Bahá'u'lláh the Day-Star of Divine guidance which, as foretold by Shaykh Ahmad and Siyyid Kázim, had risen in Shíráz, and, while pursuing its westward course, had mounted its zenith in Adrianople, had finally sunk below the horizon of 'Akká, never to rise again ere the complete revolution of one thousand years. The setting of so effulgent an Orb brought to a definite termination the period of Divine Revelation — the initial and most vitalizing stage in the Bahá'í era. Inaugurated by the Báb, culminating in Bahá'u'lláh, anticipated and extolled by the entire company of the Prophets of this great prophetic cycle, this period has, except for the short interval between the Báb's martyrdom and Bahá'u'lláh's shaking experiences in the Síyáh-Chál of Tihrán, been characterized by almost fifty years of continuous and progressive Revelation — a period which by its duration and fecundity must be regarded as unparalleled in the entire field of the world's spiritual history.

The passing of 'Abdu'l-Bahá, on the other hand, marks the closing of the Heroic and Apostolic Age of this same Dispensation — that primitive period of our Faith the splendours of which can never be rivalled, much less be eclipsed, by the magnificence that must needs distinguish the future victories of Bahá'u'lláh's Revelation. For neither the achievements of the champion-builders of the present-day institutions of the Faith of Bahá'u'lláh, nor the tumultuous triumphs which the heroes of its Golden Age will in the coming days succeed in winning, can measure with, or be included within the same category as, the wondrous works associated with the names of those who have generated its very life and laid its pristine foundations. That first and creative age of the Bahá'í era must, by its very nature, stand above and apart from the formative period into which we have entered and the golden age destined to succeed it.

'Abdu'l-Bahá, Who incarnates an institution for which we can find no parallel whatsoever in any of the world's recognized religious systems, may be said to have closed the Age to which He Himself belonged and opened the one in which we are now labouring. His Will and Testament should thus be regarded as the perpetual, the indissoluble link which the mind of Him Who is the Mystery of God has conceived in order to insure the continuity of the three ages that constitute the component parts of the Bahá'í Dispensation. The period in which the seed of the Faith had been slowly germinating is thus intertwined both with the one which must witness its efflorescence and the subsequent age in which that seed will have finally yielded its golden fruit.

The creative energies released by the Law of Bahá'u'lláh, permeating and evolving within the mind of 'Abdu'l-Bahá, have, by their very impact and close interaction, given birth to an Instrument which may be viewed as the Charter of the New World Order which is at once the glory and the promise of this most great Dispensation. The Will may thus be acclaimed as the inevitable offspring resulting from that mystic intercourse between Him Who communicated the generating influence of His divine Purpose and the One Who was its vehicle and chosen recipient. Being the Child of the Covenant — the Heir of both the Originator and the Interpreter of the Law of God — the Will and Testament of 'Abdu'l-Bahá can no more be divorced from Him Who supplied the original and motivating impulse than from the One Who ultimately conceived it. Bahá'u'lláh's inscrutable purpose, we must ever bear in mind, has been so thoroughly infused into the conduct of 'Abdu'l-Bahá, and their motives have been so closely wedded together, that the mere attempt to dissociate the teachings of the former from any system which the ideal Exemplar of those same teachings has established would amount to a repudiation of one of the most sacred and basic truths of the Faith.

The Administrative Order, which ever since 'Abdu'l-Bahá's ascension has evolved and is taking shape under our very eyes in no fewer than forty countries of the world, may be considered as the framework of the Will itself, the inviolable stronghold wherein this new-born child is being nurtured and developed. This Administrative Order, as it expands and consolidates itself, will no doubt manifest the potentialities and reveal the full implications of this momentous Document — this most remarkable expression of the Will of One of the most remarkable Figures of the Dispensation of Bahá'u'lláh. It will, as its component parts, its organic institutions, begin to function with efficiency and vigour, assert its claim and demonstrate its capacity to be regarded not only as the nucleus but the very pattern of the New World Order destined to embrace in the fulness of time the whole of mankind.

It should be noted in this connection that this Administrative Order is fundamentally different from anything that any Prophet has previously established, inasmuch as Bahá'u'lláh has Himself revealed its principles, established its institutions, appointed the person to interpret His Word and conferred the necessary authority on the body designed to supplement and apply His legislative ordinances. Therein lies the secret of its strength, its fundamental distinction, and the guarantee against disintegration and schism. Nowhere in the sacred scriptures of any of the world's religious systems, nor even in the writings of the Inaugurator of the Bábí Dispensation, do we find any provisions establishing a covenant or providing for an administrative order that can compare in scope and authority with those that lie at the very basis of the Bahá'í Dispensation. Has either Christianity or Islám, to take as an instance two of the most widely diffused and outstanding among the world's recognized religions, anything to offer that can measure with, or be regarded as equivalent to, either the Book of Bahá'u'-lláh's Covenant or to the Will and Testament of 'Abdu'l-Bahá ? Does the text of either the Gospel or the Qur'án confer sufficient authority upon those leaders and councils that have claimed the right and assumed the function of interpreting the provisions of their sacred scriptures and of administering the affairs of their respective communities ? Could Peter, the admitted chief of the Apostles, or the Imám 'Alí, the cousin and legitimate successor of the Prophet, produce in support of the primacy with which both had been invested written and explicit affirmations from Christ and Muḥammad that could have silenced those who either among their contemporaries or in a later age have repudiated their authority and, by their action, precipitated the schisms that persist until the present day ? Where, we may confidently ask, in the recorded sayings of Jesus Christ, whether in the matter of succession or in the provision of a set of specific laws and clearly defined administrative ordinances, as distinguished from purely spiritual principles, can we find anything approaching the detailed injunctions, laws and warnings that abound in the authenticated utterances of both Bahá'u'lláh and 'Abdu'l-Bahá ? Can any passage of the Qur'án, which in respect to its legal code, its administrative and devotional ordinances marks already a notable advance over previous and more corrupted Revelations, be construed as placing upon an unassailable basis the undoubted authority with which Muḥammad had, verbally and on several occasions, invested His successor ? Can the Author of the Bábí Dispensation, however much He may have succeeded through the provisions of the Persian Bayán in averting a schism as permanent and catastrophic as those that afflicted Christianity and Islám — can He be said to have produced instruments for the safeguarding of His Faith as definite and efficacious as those which must for all time preserve the unity of the organized followers of the Faith of Bahá'u'lláh ?

Alone of all the Revelations gone before it this Faith has, through the explicit directions, the repeated warnings, the authenticated safeguards incorporated and elaborated in its teachings, succeeded in raising a structure which the bewildered followers of bankrupt and broken creeds might well approach and critically examine, and seek, ere it is too late, the invulnerable security of its world-embracing shelter.

No wonder that He Who through the operation of His Will has inaugurated so vast and unique an Order and Who is the Centre of so mighty a Covenant should have written these words : " *So firm and mighty is this Covenant that from the beginning of time until the present day no religious Dispensation hath produced its like.*" " *Whatsoever is latent in the innermost of this holy cycle,*" He wrote during the darkest and most dangerous days of His ministry, " *shall gradually appear and be made manifest, for now is but the beginning of its growth and the day-spring of the revelation of its signs.*"

" *Fear not*," are His reassuring words foreshadowing the rise of the Administrative Order established by His Will, " *fear not if this Branch be severed from this material world and cast aside its leaves ; nay, the leaves thereof shall flourish, for this Branch will grow after it is cut off from this world below, it shall reach the loftiest pinnacles of glory, and it shall bear such fruits as will perfume the world with their fragrance.*"

To what else if not to the power and majesty which this Administrative Order — the rudiments of the future all-enfolding Bahá'í Commonwealth — is destined to manifest, can these utterances of Bahá'u'lláh allude ; " *The world's equilibrium hath been upset through the vibrating influence of this most great, this new World Order. Mankind's ordered life hath been revolutionized through the agency of this unique, this wondrous System — the like of which mortal eyes have never witnessed.*"

The Báb Himself, in the course of His references to " Him Whom God will make manifest " anticipates the System and glorifies the World Order which the Revelation of Bahá'u'lláh is destined to unfold. " *Well is it with him,*" is His remarkable statement in the third chapter of the Persian Bayán, " *who fixeth his gaze upon the Order of Bahá'u'lláh and rendereth thanks unto his Lord ! For He will assuredly be made manifest. God hath indeed irrevocably ordained it in the Bayán.*"

In the Tablets of Bahá'u'lláh where the institutions of the International and Local Houses of Justice are specifically designated and formally established ; in the institution of the Hands of the Cause of God which first Bahá'u'lláh and then 'Abdu'l-Bahá brought into being ; in the institution of both local and national Assemblies which in their embryonic stage were already functioning in the days preceding 'Abdu'l-Bahá's ascension ; in the authority with which the Author of our Faith and the Centre of His Covenant have in their Tablets chosen to confer upon them ; in the institution of the Local Fund which operated according to 'Abdu'l-Bahá's specific injunctions addressed to certain Assemblies in Persia ; in the verses of the Kitáb-i-Aqdas the implications of which clearly anticipate the institution of the Guardianship ; in the explanation which 'Abdu'l-Bahá, in one of His Tablets, has given to, and the emphasis He has placed upon, the hereditary principle and the law of primogeniture as having been upheld by the Prophets of the past — in these we can discern the faint glimmerings and discover the earliest intimation of the nature and working of the Administrative Order which the Will of 'Abdu'l-Bahá was at a later time destined to proclaim and formally establish.

An attempt, I feel, should at the present juncture be made to explain the character and functions of the twin pillars that support this mighty Administrative Structure — the institutions of the Guardianship and of the Universal House of Justice. To describe in their entirety the diverse elements that function in conjunction with these institutions is beyond the scope and purpose of this general exposition of the fundamental verities of the Faith. To define with accuracy and minuteness the features, and to analyze exhaustively the nature of the relationships which, on the one hand, bind together these two fundamental organs of the Will of 'Abdu'l-Bahá and connect, on the other, each of them to the Author of the Faith and the Centre of His Covenant is a task which future generations will no doubt adequately fulfil. My present intention is to elaborate certain salient features of this scheme which, however close we may stand to its colossal structure, are already so clearly defined that we find it inexcusable to either misconceive or ignore.

It should be stated, at the very outset, in clear and unambiguous language, that these twin institutions of the Administrative Order of Bahá'u'lláh should be regarded as divine in origin, essential in their functions and complementary in their aim and purpose. Their common, their fundamental object is to insure the continuity of that divinely-appointed authority which flows from the Source of our Faith, to safeguard the unity of its followers and to maintain the integrity and flexibility of its teachings. Acting in conjunction with each other these two inseparable institutions administer its affairs, co-ordinate its activities, promote its interests, execute its laws and defend its subsidiary institutions. Severally, each operates within a clearly defined sphere of jurisdiction; each is equipped with its own attendant institutions — instruments designed for the effective discharge of its particular responsibilities and duties. Each exercises, within the limitations imposed upon it, its powers, its authority, its rights and prerogatives. These are neither contradictory, nor detract in the slightest degree from the position which each of these institutions occupies. Far from being incompatible or mutually destructive, they supplement each other's authority and functions, and are permanently and fundamentally united in their aims.

Divorced from the institution of the Guardianship the World Order of Bahá'u'lláh would be mutilated and permanently deprived of that hereditary principle which, as 'Abdu'l-Bahá has written, has been invariably upheld by the Law of God. " *In all the Divine Dispensations*," He states, in a Tablet addressed to a follower of the Faith in Persia, " *the eldest son hath been given extraordinary distinctions. Even the station of prophethood hath been his birthright.*" Without such an institution the integrity of the Faith would be imperilled, and the stability of the entire fabric would be gravely endangered. Its prestige would suffer, the means required to enable it to take a long, an uninterrupted view over a series of generations would be completely lacking, and the necessary guidance to define the sphere of the legislative action of its elected representatives would be totally withdrawn.

Severed from the no less essential institution of the Universal House of Justice this same System of the Will of 'Abdu'l-Bahá would be paralyzed in its action and would be powerless to fill in those gaps which the Author of the Kitáb-i-Aqdas has deliberately left in the body of His legislative and administrative ordinances.

" *He is the Interpreter of the Word of God*," 'Abdu'l-Bahá, referring to the functions of the Guardian of the Faith, asserts, using in His Will the very term which He Himself had chosen when refuting the argument of the Covenant-breakers who had challenged His right to interpret the utterances of Bahá'u'lláh. " *After him*," He adds, " *will succeed the first-born of his lineal descendants.*" " *The mighty stronghold*," He further explains, " *shall remain impregnable and safe through obedience to him who is the Guardian of the Cause of God." " It is incumbent upon the members of the House of Justice, upon all the Agh̲sán, the Afnán, the Hands of the Cause of God, to show their obedience, submissiveness and subordination unto the Guardian of the Cause of God."*

" *It is incumbent upon the members of the House of Justice,*" Bahá'u'lláh, on the other hand, declares in the Eighth Leaf of the Exalted Paradise, " *to take counsel together regarding those things which have not outwardly been revealed in the Book, and to enforce that which is agreeable to them. God will verily inspire them with whatsoever He willeth, and He verily is the Provider, the Omniscient.*" "*Unto the Most Holy Book*" (the Kitáb-i-Aqdas), 'Abdu'l-Bahá states in His Will, " *every one must turn, and all that is not expressly recorded therein must be referred to the Universal House of Justice. That which this body, whether unanimously or by a majority doth carry, that is verily the truth and the purpose of God Himself. Whoso doth deviate therefrom is verily of them that love discord, hath shown forth malice, and turned away from the Lord of the covenant.*"

Not only does 'Abdu'l-Bahá confirm in His Will Bahá'u'lláh's above-quoted statement, but invests this body with the additional right and power to abrogate, according to the exigencies of time, its own enactments, as well as those of a preceding House of Justice. " *Inasmuch as the House of Justice,*" is His explicit statement in His Will, " *hath power to enact laws that are not expressly recorded in the Book and bear upon daily transactions, so also it hath power to repeal the same . . . This it can do because these laws form no part of the divine explicit text.*"

Referring to both the Guardian and the Universal House of Justice we read these emphatic words : " *The sacred and youthful Branch, the Guardian of the Cause of God, as well as the Universal House of Justice to be universally elected and established, are both under the care and protection of the Abhá Beauty, under the shelter and unerring guidance of the Exalted One* (the Báb) (*may my life be offered up for them both*). *Whatsoever they decide is of God.*"

From these statements it is made indubitably clear and evident that the Guardian of the Faith has been made the Interpreter of the Word and that the Universal House of Justice has been invested with the function of legislating on matters not expressly revealed in the teachings. The interpretation of the Guardian, functioning within his own sphere, is as authoritative and binding as the enactments of the International House of Justice, whose exclusive right and prerogative is to pronounce upon and deliver the final judgment on such laws and ordinances as Bahá'u'lláh has not expressly revealed. Neither can, nor will ever, infringe upon the sacred and prescribed domain of the other. Neither will seek to curtail the specific and undoubted authority with which both have been divinely invested.

Though the Guardian of the Faith has been made the permanent head of so august a body he can never, even temporarily, assume the right of exclusive legislation. He cannot override the decision of the majority of his fellow-members, but is bound to insist upon a reconsideration by them of any enactment he conscientiously believes to conflict with the meaning and to depart from the spirit of Bahá'u'lláh's revealed utterances. He interprets what has been specifically revealed, and cannot legislate except in his capacity as member of the Universal House of Justice. He is debarred from laying down independently the constitution that must govern the organized activities of his fellow-members, and from exercising his influence in a manner that would encroach upon the liberty of those whose sacred right is to elect the body of his collaborators.

It should be borne in mind that the institution of the Guardianship has been anticipated by 'Abdu'l-Bahá in an allusion He made in a Tablet addressed, long before His own ascension, to three of His friends in Persia. To their question as to whether there would be any person to whom all the Bahá'ís would be called upon to turn after His ascension He made the following reply : " *As to the question ye have asked me, know verily that this is a well-guarded secret. It is even as a gem concealed within its shell. That it will be revealed is predestined. The time will come when its light will appear, when its evidences will be made manifest, and its secrets unravelled.*"

Dearly-beloved friends ! Exalted as is the position and vital as is the function of the institution of the Guardianship in the Administrative Order of Bahá'u'lláh, and staggering as must be the weight of responsibility which it carries, its importance must, whatever be the language of the Will, be in no wise over-emphasized. The Guardian of the Faith must not under any circumstances, and whatever his merits or his achievements, be exalted to the rank that will make him a co-sharer with 'Abdu'l-Bahá in the unique position which the Centre of the Covenant occupies — much less to the station exclusively ordained for the Manifestation of God. So grave a departure from the established tenets of our Faith is nothing short of open blasphemy. As I have already stated, in the course of my references to 'Abdu'l-Bahá's station, however great the gulf that separates Him from the Author of a Divine Revelation it can never measure with the distance that stands between Him Who is the Centre of Bahá'u'lláh's Covenant and the Guardians who are its chosen ministers. There is a far, far greater distance separating the Guardian from the Centre of the Covenant than there is between the Centre of the Covenant and its Author.

No Guardian of the Faith, I feel it my solemn duty to place on record, can ever claim to be the perfect exemplar of the teachings of Bahá'u'lláh or the stainless mirror that reflects His light. Though overshadowed by the unfailing, the unerring protection of Bahá'u'lláh and of the Báb, and however much he may share with 'Abdu'l-Bahá the right and obligation to interpret the Bahá'í teachings, he remains essentially human and cannot, if he wishes to remain faithful to his trust, arrogate to himself, under any pretence whatsoever, the rights, the privileges and prerogatives which Bahá'u'lláh has chosen to confer upon His Son. In the light of this truth to pray to the Guardian of the Faith, to address him as lord and master, to designate him as his holiness, to seek his benediction, to celebrate his birthday, or to commemorate any event associated with his life would be tantamount to a departure from those established truths that are enshrined within our beloved Faith. The fact that the Guardian has been specifically endowed with such power as he may need to reveal the purport and disclose the implications of the utterances of Bahá'u'lláh and of 'Abdu'l-Bahá does not necessarily confer upon him a station co-equal with those Whose words he is called upon to interpret. He can exercise that right and discharge this obligation and yet remain infinitely inferior to both of them in rank and different in nature.

To the integrity of this cardinal principle of our Faith the words, the deeds of its present and future Guardians must abundantly testify. By their conduct and example they must needs establish its truth upon an unassailable foundation and transmit to future generations unimpeachable evidences of its reality.

For my own part to hesitate in recognizing so vital a truth or to vacillate in proclaiming so firm a conviction must constitute a shameless betrayal of the confidence reposed in me by 'Abdu'l-Bahá and an unpardonable usurpation of the authority with which He Himself has been invested.

A word should now be said regarding the theory on which this Administrative Order is based and the principle that must govern the operation of its chief institutions. It would be utterly misleading to attempt a comparison between this unique, this divinely-conceived Order and any of the diverse systems which the minds of men, at various periods of their history, have contrived for the government of human institutions. Such an attempt would in itself betray a lack of complete appreciation of the excellence of the handiwork of its great Author. How could it be otherwise when we remember that this Order constitutes the very pattern of that divine civilization which the almighty Law of Bahá'u'lláh is designed to establish upon earth? The divers and ever-shifting systems of human polity, whether past or present, whether originating in the East or in the West, offer no adequate criterion wherewith to estimate the potency of its hidden virtues or to appraise the solidity of its foundations.

The Bahá'í Commonwealth of the future, of which this vast Administrative Order is the sole framework, is, both in theory and

practice, not only unique in the entire history of political institutions, but can find no parallel in the annals of any of the world's
recognized religious systems. No form of democratic government ;
no system of autocracy or of dictatorship, whether monarchical or
republican ; no intermediary scheme of a purely aristocratic order ;
nor even any of the recognized types of theocracy, whether it be
the Hebrew Commonwealth, or the various Christian ecclesiastical
organizations, or the Imamate or the Caliphate in Islám — none of
these can be identified or be said to conform with the Administrative Order which the master-hand of its perfect Architect has
fashioned.

This new-born Administrative Order incorporates within its
structure certain elements which are to be found in each of the
three recognized forms of secular government, without being in
any sense a mere replica of any one of them, and without intro-
ducing within its machinery any of the objectionable features
which they inherently possess. It blends and harmonizes, as no
government fashioned by mortal hands has as yet accomplished,
the salutary truths which each of these systems undoubtedly con-
tains without vitiating the integrity of those God-given verities on
which it is ultimately founded.

The Administrative Order of the Faith of Bahá'u'lláh must in
no wise be regarded as purely democratic in character inasmuch as
the basic assumption which requires all democracies to depend
fundamentally upon getting their mandate from the people is
altogether lacking in this Dispensation. In the conduct of the
administrative affairs of the Faith, in the enactment of the legislation necessary to supplement the laws of the Kitáb-i-Aqdas, the
members of the Universal House of Justice, it should be borne in
mind, are not, as Bahá'u'lláh's utterances clearly imply, responsible
to those whom they represent, nor are they allowed to be governed
by the feelings, the general opinion, and even the convictions of the
mass of the faithful, or of those who directly elect them. They are
to follow, in a prayerful attitude, the dictates and promptings of
their conscience. They may, indeed they must, acquaint themselves with the conditions prevailing among the community, must

weigh dispassionately in their minds the merits of any case present-
ed for their consideration, but must reserve for themselves the
right of an unfettered decision. " *God will verily inspire them with
whatsoever He willeth,*" is Bahá'u'lláh's incontrovertible assurance.
They, and not the body of those who either directly or indirectly
elect them, have thus been made the recipients of the divine
guidance which is at once the life-blood and ultimate safeguard of
this Revelation. Moreover, he who symbolizes the hereditary
principle in this Dispensation has been made the interpreter of the
words of its Author, and ceases consequently, by virtue of the actual
authority vested in him, to be the figurehead invariably associated
with the prevailing systems of constitutional monarchies.

Nor can the Bahá'í Administrative Order be dismissed as a
hard and rigid system of unmitigated autocracy or as an idle imi-
tation of any form of absolutistic ecclesiastical government, whether
it be the Papacy, the Imamate or any other similar institution, for
the obvious reason that upon the international elected representatives of the followers of Bahá'u'lláh has been conferred the exclusive right of legislating on matters not expressly revealed in the
Bahá'í writings. Neither the Guardian of the Faith nor any
institution apart from the International House of Justice can ever
usurp this vital and essential power or encroach upon that sacred
right. The abolition of professional priesthood with its accom-
panying sacraments of baptism, of communion and of confession
of sins, the laws requiring the election by universal suffrage of all
local, national, and international Houses of Justice, the total absence
of episcopal authority with its attendant privileges, corruptions and
bureaucratic tendencies, are further evidences of the non-auto-
cratic character of the Bahá'í Administrative Order and of its
inclination to democratic methods in the administration of its
affairs.

Nor is this Order identified with the name of Bahá'u'lláh to
be confused with any system of purely aristocratic government in
view of the fact that it upholds, on the one hand, the hereditary
principle and entrusts the Guardian of the Faith with the obligation of interpreting its teachings, and provides, on the other, for

the free and direct election from among the mass of the faithful of the body that constitutes its highest legislative organ.

Whereas this Administrative Order cannot be said to have been modelled after any of these recognized systems of government, it nevertheless embodies, reconciles and assimilates within its framework such wholesome elements as are to be found in each one of them. The hereditary authority which the Guardian is called upon to exercise, the vital and essential functions which the Universal House of Justice discharges, the specific provisions requiring its democratic election by the representatives of the faithful — these combine to demonstrate the truth that this divinely revealed Order, which can never be identified with any of the standard types of government referred to by Aristotle in his works, embodies and blends with the spiritual verities on which it is based the beneficent elements which are to be found in each one of them. The admitted evils inherent in each of these systems being rigidly and permanently excluded, this unique Order, however long it may endure and however extensive its ramifications, cannot ever degenerate into any form of despotism, of oligarchy, or of demagogy which must sooner or later corrupt the machinery of all man-made and essentially defective political institutions.

Dearly-beloved friends ! Significant as are the origins of this mighty administrative structure, and however unique its features, the happenings that may be said to have heralded its birth and signalized the initial stage of its evolution seem no less remarkable. How striking, how edifying the contrast between the process of slow and steady consolidation that characterizes the growth of its infant strength and the devastating onrush of the forces of disintegration that are assailing the outworn institutions, both religious and secular, of present-day society !

The vitality which the organic institutions of this great, this ever-expanding Order so strongly exhibit ; the obstacles which the high courage, the undaunted resolution of its administrators have already surmounted ; the fire of an unquenchable enthusiasm that glows with undiminished fervour in the hearts of its itinerant teachers ; the heights of self-sacrifice which its champion-builders are now attaining ; the breadth of vision, the confident hope, the creative joy, the inward peace, the uncompromising integrity, the exemplary discipline, the unyeilding unity and solidarity which its stalwart defenders manifest ; the degree to which its moving Spirit has shown itself capable of assimilating the diversified elements within its pale, of cleansing them of all forms of prejudice and of fusing them with its own structure — these are evidences of a power which a disillusioned and sadly shaken society can ill afford to ignore.

Compare these splendid manifestations of the spirit animating this vibrant body of the Faith of Bahá'u'lláh with the cries and agony, the follies and vanities, the bitterness and prejudices, the wickedness and divisions of an ailing and chaotic world. Witness the fear that torments its leaders and paralyzes the action of its blind and bewildered statesmen. How fierce the hatreds, how false the ambitions, how petty the pursuits, how deep-rooted the suspicions of its peoples ! How disquieting the lawlessness, the corruption, the unbelief that are eating into the vitals of a tottering civilization !

Might not this process of steady deterioration which is insidiously invading so many departments of human activity and thought be regarded as a necessary accompaniment to the rise of this almighty Arm of Bahá'u'lláh ? Might we not look upon the momentous happenings which, in the course of the past twenty years, have so deeply agitated every continent of the earth, as ominous signs simultaneously proclaiming the agonies of a disintegrating civilization and the birthpangs of that World Order — that Ark of human salvation — that must needs arise upon its ruins ?

The catastrophic fall of mighty monarchies and empires in the European continent, allusions to some of which may be found in the prophecies of Bahá'u'lláh ; the decline that has set in, and is still continuing, in the fortunes of the Shí'ih hierarchy in His own native land ; the fall of the Qájár dynasty, the traditional enemy of His Faith ; the overthrow of the Sultanate and the Caliphate, the sustaining pillars of Sunní Islám, to which the destruction of Jerusalem in the latter part of the first century of the Christian era offers a striking parallel ; the wave of secularization which is invading the Muḥammadan ecclesiastical institutions in Egypt and sapping the loyalty of its staunchest supporters ; the humiliating blows that have afflicted some of the most powerful Churches of Christendom in Russia, in Western Europe and Central America ; the dissemination of those subversive doctrines that are undermining the foundations and overthrowing the structure of seemingly impregnable strongholds in the political and social spheres of human activity ; the signs of an impending catastrophe, strangely reminiscent of the Fall of the Roman Empire in the West, which threatens to engulf the whole structure of present-day civilization — all witness to the tumult which the birth of this mighty Organ of the Religion of Bahá'u'lláh has cast into the world — a tumult which will grow in scope and in intensity as the implications of this constantly evolving Scheme are more fully understood and its ramifications more widely extended over the surface of the globe.

A word more in conclusion. The rise and establishment of this Administrative Order — the shell that shields and enshrines so precious a gem — constitutes the hall-mark of this second and formative age of the Bahá'í era. It will come to be regarded, as it recedes farther and farther from our eyes, as the chief agency empowered to usher in the concluding phase, the consummation of this glorious Dispensation.

Let no one, while this System is still in its infancy, misconceive its character, belittle its significance or misrepresent its purpose. The bedrock on which this Administrative Order is founded is God's immutable Purpose for mankind in this day. The Source from which it derives its inspiration is no one less than Bahá'u'lláh Himself. Its shield and defender are the embattled hosts of the Abhá Kingdom. Its seed is the blood of no less than twenty thousand martyrs who have offered up their lives that it may be born and flourish. The axis round which its institutions revolve are the authentic provisions of the Will and Testament of 'Abdu'l-

Bahá. Its guiding principles are the truths which He Who is the unerring Interpreter of the teachings of our Faith has so clearly enunciated in His public addresses throughout the West. The laws that govern its operation and limit its functions are those which have been expressly ordained in the Kitáb-i-Aqdas. The seat round which its spiritual, its humanitarian and administrative activities will cluster are the Mashriqu'l-Adhkár and its Dependencies. The pillars that sustain its authority and buttress its structure are the twin institutions of the Guardianship and of the Universal House of Justice. The central, the underlying aim which animates it is the establishment of the New World Order as adumbrated by Bahá'u'lláh. The methods it employs, the standard it inculcates, incline it to neither East nor West, neither Jew nor Gentile, neither rich nor poor, neither white nor coloured. Its watchword is the unification of the human race ; its standard the " Most Great Peace " ; its consummation the advent of that golden millennium — the Day when the kingdoms of this world shall have become the Kingdom of God Himself, the Kingdom of Bahá'u'lláh.

SHOGHI.

Haifa, Palestine,
February 8, 1934.

OTHER WRITINGS BY SHOGHI EFFENDI